THRIFTY TEACHER'S GUIDE

to Creative Learning Centers

by Shelley Nicholson, PhD, and Jessica Martinez

Gryphon House
www.gryphonhouse.com

Bulk Purchase
Gryphon House books are available for special premiums and sales promotions as well as for fund-raising use. Special editions or book excerpts also can be created to specifications. For details, call 800.638.0928.

Disclaimer
Gryphon House, Inc., cannot be held responsible for damage, mishap, or injury incurred during the use of or because of activities in this book. Appropriate and reasonable caution and adult supervision of children involved in activities and corresponding to the age and capability of each child involved are recommended at all times. Do not leave children unattended at any time. Observe safety and caution at all times.

Dedication

We dedicate this book to thrifty teachers everywhere, and to our mothers, Mary Jane Martinez and Penny Atkinson Redmon.

Acknowledgments

Both of us have been fortunate to work with many creative and talented teachers, and we appreciate the collaboration and support they have provided that encouraged us to pursue writing this book. We thank our colleagues at Nicholson Early Childhood Education Center and The Goddard School of Austin, Texas, for supporting us and sharing our passion. A special thanks to Kate Palmer, Linda Crossman, Monica Holder, June Hall, Alysia Lopez, Isa and Raul Alvarez, Malorie Looney, and Heather Duran.

We are also very grateful to Dr. Stuart Reifel and Renita Pizzitola for treasured early feedback as well as technical and moral support.

We would like to thank everyone at Gryphon House for taking a chance on us and helping us turn our dream into a reality!

And finally, a huge thank you to our families and friends for their support, encouragement, and patience with our hoarding tendencies! Specifically, Jessica would like to thank Edward Murray for supporting her 110 percent and being her number-one fan. Shelley would like to thank Shawn and Allen for always being wonderfully supportive.

Table of Contents

Introduction

In our quest as early childhood educators to provide high-quality and enriching environments for young children, we recognize that the materials we choose play an important role in children's learning and development. The challenge for many teachers is to create and maintain these environments with the limited resources available. Most early childhood programs have modest budgets for purchasing new materials, but even if teachers were allowed to make unrestricted purchases, most would likely become bored and frustrated with the choices offered through mainstream educational suppliers. Children often have more fun—and seem to learn more—when playing with the box a toy came in rather than the toy itself!

Early childhood research (for example, Frost, Wortham, and Reifel, 2012; Van Hoorn et al., 2012) tells us that, when given the opportunity to play with open-ended materials, children are afforded some of their greatest learning opportunities. Open-ended materials provide inspiration for the young child's imagination. A simple box can become a doll's bed or a treasure chest full of booty for pirates. A collection of boxes can become a set of building blocks. When you begin to use your imagination in this way, you will see the potential to turn common and recycled objects into play and learning materials for your classroom.

Our purpose with this book is to demonstrate a multitude of ways that you can easily and inexpensively collect and create a great variety of open-ended learning materials for your preschool learning environment. As early childhood educators ourselves, we are particularly interested in the use of materials to support learning through play. Research continues to confirm the crucial role of play in children's early education, and providing opportunities for open-ended play is a central tenet in the framework for best practices in our field (Copple and Bredekamp, 2009). You can promote learning by providing time within your daily schedules for play and by creating environments that invite children to engage in play.

In the pages that follow, you will find ideas for both collecting common or recycled materials for your classroom as well as ideas for creating materials with the goal of inspiring specific types of play and learning.

1 Creating and Implementing Imaginative Learning Centers

LEARNING THROUGH PLAY WITH MATERIALS

Researchers have shown that play has both direct and indirect influences on children's learning and development (Trawick-Smith, 2009). You can observe some of the direct learning benefits of play when you see children using language to interact socially with others during dramatic play, when they problem-solve how to keep a block tower from tumbling, or when they utilize their fine-motor skills to complete a puzzle. Indirect benefits, such as progress in self-regulatory skills, building attention span, or learning to create symbols in their play, are more difficult to recognize without a broad understanding of the ways that play contributes to learning. Play with materials provides an avenue for all of these learning possibilities. When you provide time and opportunity for play, you are using it as a powerful medium of instruction.

We enjoy the metaphor that portrays classroom materials as children's textbooks (Cuffaro, 1995). It is clear that children need to interact physically with objects such as blocks to gain their foundational understandings of physics and geometry. They are introduced to the world of literature by exploring books and enacting stories with puppets or props. They learn to sort and manipulate objects, which sets the stage for later arithmetic. Open-ended opportunities with a variety of paper, art materials, and writing utensils are how learning to be an author or an artist begins. In fact, a defining feature of any early childhood program is the materials chosen. Regardless of the philosophy or the curriculum approach utilized, materials matter.

Research suggests that balance in the variety of play materials made available to children will lead them to deeper levels of engagement and provides them with greater opportunities for learning (Prescott, 1987, 1994). One way that you can promote this balance is to include both open-ended and closed materials in the learning environment. Open-ended materials, such as blocks or playdough, are those that children can use in multiple ways; whereas, closed materials, such as a puzzle, typically have just a single function. Both types of materials are valuable but serve different purposes (Guilford, 1957). Open-ended materials allow children to explore, create, and search for multiple solutions to any problems they create or encounter. Closed materials require children to find the best solution to a problem or the one right answer.

In this book, we have chosen to focus primarily on open-ended materials and activities because of the learning possibilities they possess. Children are free to direct their own actions. Even some materials that might be considered closed can be utilized in a variety of ways if children are permitted to direct their own actions while using them. For example, if a child finds an animal bingo game that has been set out on a table, but he is the only one who seems interested at the moment, he might begin lining up the animal cards and have them talk to each other. When children have a portion of time in the day to make their own choices, the possibilities for creative play are endless.

Some open-ended materials can provide opportunities for learning in a specific domain. For example, a teacher hoping to enhance children's fine-motor skills might introduce more manipulative materials in her classroom, such as finger-sliding trays or puzzles. Ultimately, when children are interacting with materials in an open-ended fashion, it is hard to guess how they might end up using them.

CREATING THE ENVIRONMENT AND ROTATING MATERIALS

In many curriculum philosophies, the teacher is first seen as the creator of the environment. He designs the classroom space and chooses the materials. Many teachers arrange their furnishings to create centers or areas with particular materials that are related to one another. Research has found that when classrooms are arranged in this manner, children tend to play longer, which ultimately leads to higher levels of thinking (Moore, 2002). While there is variation in the names used for different centers and how they are arranged and combined, the most common classroom learning centers include dramatic play, blocks, library, art, writing, science, sensory, math, manipulatives, and music. Teachers typically stock these areas with materials specific to those categories and then add, rotate, and replace materials based on either a changing curriculum theme or, in the case of emergent approaches, the children's interests.

Observe children's play to gain the best information about when to make changes to the environment. As you observe, ask yourself questions such as the following:

- What materials are holding the children's interests?
- What new interests do the children have that are not yet supported by materials?
- What themes do I see in the children's play?
- What materials or props might I add to support their play themes?
- What materials have not been played with recently?
- Are there too many choices in the environment?
- Are there too few choices?

Open-ended materials are fluid. Children will often use materials in novel ways or move them from one area in the classroom to another to serve their purposes. Wooden blocks may be taken to the dramatic play area to become cans of food for a grocery store. A picnic basket of play food may be carried to the block area that has imaginatively become a field of flowers. When you allow children to use materials in the manner they choose, the materials can support a multitude of learning opportunities.

You might purposefully place materials in unexpected areas to promote different experiences. For example, Ping-Pong balls placed in the block center might promote rolling on ramps, while Ping-Pong balls placed in the dramatic play area might promote scooping of pretend ice cream. Open-ended materials in particular provide for greater fluidity and creativity in how children use them.

In addition to providing and rotating materials, it is important to ensure that children have access to materials that they can use to create their own materials and props for play. Younger preschoolers may not yet be able to create their own props, but older preschoolers will be inspired by your creativity to make their own creations. A bin of recycled boxes and tubes placed near general art supplies will most likely lead to amazing creations!

INVITING CHILDREN TO PLAY

In most early childhood classrooms, materials are available on low shelving so that children can access them without assistance from adults. Teachers often prepare their classroom environments by selecting materials to set on tabletops or by creating displays on the tops of shelves or even on the floors. Within some curriculum philosophies, specific terms such as *invitations* or *provocations* are used to describe the way that teachers purposefully set up the environment to entice children to play with and explore materials. For example, a teacher might set a table in the dramatic-play area to inspire sociodramatic play. Or she might set baskets of objects on a table along with a balance scale to invite exploration of weight. The arrangement and presentation of materials can play a role in helping children become engaged in classroom activity.

Teachers often work to make their classroom aesthetically pleasing to children, and this includes the arrangement of materials. Items can be stored and displayed in a variety of baskets, boxes, tubs, or trays. You can set up areas in ways that encourage social interactions or that allow for solitary activity. In addition to how the materials are presented, you may also want to ensure that children can make their choices independently. This might include providing tools for self-help such as small brooms and dustpans so that children can clean up after themselves, or paint smocks hanging where children can reach.

ENGAGING WITH CHILDREN DURING PLAY

Depending on your program's philosophy, your role in relation to the children interacting with materials will vary. You might just observe the children to develop greater understandings about their development. You might join in when you see a teachable moment. You might lead the children in a specific task to promote a specific curriculum goal.

Reflective teaching practices will assist you in making decisions about when to step in to children's play and when it is best to let the moment unfold at the children's direction. With the best of intentions, sometimes teachers interrupt children at play when the concepts or skills they are learning in that moment might be more beneficial for them than what the teacher had intended to teach. Before jumping in, just observe for a moment or two to see what is happening. You might see the perfect opportunity to add to what is happening and introduce new vocabulary or to pose an open-ended question, but make these decisions purposefully and individualize them to the children's specific needs and development.

ENHANCING THE LEARNING ENVIRONMENT WITH MATERIALS

Other than purchasing new materials, we see three primary ways that teachers can enhance their learning environments:

- **Teachers might rotate materials within their school.** Many schools have a supply closet or central location for storing extra materials, and teachers are able to use those in their classrooms. Teachers might also ask other teachers about borrowing or trading materials such as puzzles or books.

- **Teachers might collect materials.** For example, parents might donate discarded clothing to be used for dress-up and dramatic play. A teacher might bring in rocks or leaves from her own backyard or might save items meant for the recycling bin, such as cardboard boxes or bottle caps. These materials can be used in the classroom as they are, or to create other materials.

- **Teachers might create materials.** Using those recycled materials or simple craft supplies, teachers can create all sorts of engaging classroom materials and props for play.

FROM TRASH TO TREASURE

The hunt for free or inexpensive materials is part of the fun for many teachers. The following list provides inspiration for where you might begin:

- Clean out your closet to find gently used dress-up clothes, shoes, and bags.

- Ask classroom parents and your own family members to remember you when they clean out their closets.

- Borrow pots, pans, measuring cups, and other utensils from your own kitchen.

- What businesses are your friends and family in? Could they provide cast-off materials or loose parts?

- Save objects that some people think are trash.

- Repurpose objects from recycling bins.

- Be on the lookout for packaging materials such as sturdy cardboard mailing tubes or Styrofoam or molded-pulp braces from items shipped in boxes.

- Search the web for images and photos to enhance your materials. (Of course, you will want to obey copyright laws!)

- Talk to the managers of your favorite restaurants about donating menus, paper products, hats, or other materials.

- Some businesses will donate outdated computer paper or envelopes.

- Watch for manufacturing surplus events, as these often offer free materials such as carpet squares, tiles, or fabric.

- Visit a dollar store or the clearance aisles in discount stores.

- Stop at garage sales.

- Shop at Goodwill, Salvation Army, or thrift stores.

Safety First

It is extremely important that you make safe choices when choosing materials. A good rule of thumb is to verify with your administrators that the materials you choose are acceptable, particularly when you bring in materials that have not been used in your environment previously. The materials suggested in this book are intended for use in preschool classrooms and are not intended for children under three years of age.

CREATING MATERIALS

There are all sorts of ways to create durable materials and props to support open-ended play. In this book, we have included photos of teacher-made materials, nearly all of which were created using a wide variety of recycled materials. For some teachers, making materials is a creative outlet, and a cardboard box becomes a barn complete with red paint and white tape. But an unpainted box with a door cut into it can also be a barn. You do not need specialized training or skills in the arts or hours of time to create props. Simple, quickly made materials are wonderful, too, and children will reap the benefits.

In the interest of time, you can make good use of technology. If, for example, you want to make a matching game but only have one set of images

ANTI-BIAS MATERIALS

Enrich your learning environment with real objects, such as household items, and make materials that include diverse images of real people, food, textiles, and architecture. While it is not possible to portray the vast diversity of human life in any one classroom, consider the following categories as suggested by Derman-Sparks and Edwards (2010) when working, to ensure that many people and cultures are represented:

- The children, families, and staff in the program
- Children and families from various racial or ethnic groups
- Diversity in family structures
- Elderly people of various backgrounds performing different types of activities
- Both women and men doing jobs in the home and outside the home
- People doing all different kinds of work
- People of various backgrounds with different abilities and challenges
- Creative artwork of artists of diverse backgrounds and cultures
- Economic-class diversity
- Architecture from near and far
- Portrayals that accurately reflect people's current daily lives
- Important people, both past and present, including people who participated in important struggles for social justice
- Samples from a variety of languages including American Sign Language and Braille

available, use a color copier to make the set. A bingo grid is easy to create using the table function in a word-processing program. Save your work in an electronic folder so that you can easily reproduce a well-loved item. You can also save time by searching for free photos or images. Just search for "free photos for teachers" to find royalty-free images. **Tip:** If you need an image of an object by itself, such as an apple not attached to a tree, try searching "apple with white background."

While most teacher-made materials do not last forever, you can make the most of your work by laminating it or covering it with clear contact paper or clear, wide tape. This also works well for materials made from cardboard boxes. And, you can use page protectors when making books.

Children respond differently to realistic images versus cartoon-like drawings, and they play differently with real objects (Trawick-Smith, 1993; McLoyd, 1983). You can find photos in a variety of places such as magazines, post cards, calendars, store advertisements, recycled books, or encyclopedias, or you can take your own photographs.

By incorporating the alphabet and numerals into your teacher-made materials where appropriate, you can further enhance the children's literacy-rich environment. Many teacher-made materials inherently include literacy and math elements, but you can make further contributions by thinking specifically about these components when constructing materials. Teacher-made materials also provide the perfect opportunity to introduce examples of your own handwriting into the classroom environment.

Many teachers desire to have children's art and writing samples visible in their classrooms but have limited wall space or bulletin boards. Teacher-made materials offer countless possibilities for incorporating children's work: making books of children's artwork for the bookshelf, laminating children's work for dramatic play placemats or playdough mats, or decorating teacher-made blocks with children's work.

NOTHING NEW UNDER THE SUN?

We find inspiration from history, other teachers, the Internet, conferences, curriculum resources, educational-resource catalogs, and life! In the pages that follow, you may see many familiar teacher-made objects. During our careers, we have seen many wonderful examples. Often we will see something that reminds us of things we made in the past, and we are then inspired to make the items again. Sometimes we will see something and think about how we might add our own twist to it. Regardless, this book is just the tip of the iceberg. We look forward to seeing how you might use it to spark your own creations and the children's imaginations!

2 Blocks and Props

A preschool teacher places red cups on the shelf in the block area and watches how the children incorporate them into their play throughout the week. The first day, she notices how two girls use the cups as podiums as they pretend that toy animals are performing tricks by jumping or diving into pools that the girls created with wooden blocks. Another day, she observes a group of children building a castle with wooden blocks and using the cups as turrets on the corners of their structure. On a different occasion, she watches a child alternating cups and blocks when creating a tower. The teacher is fascinated by how a simple prop can enhance the children's block play.

Blocks have become a staple in early childhood classrooms because building is a treasured activity among young children. Beyond the pleasure of creating, blocks provide countless opportunities for learning. Not only do children explore physical properties such as size, shape, weight, and symmetry, but they also work with friends to plan, negotiate, and problem-solve. In block play, you can observe progression and increasing complexity in children's actions. The youngest children can be seen toting and carrying blocks, and they often delight in dumping and refilling buckets. In the early preschool years, you begin to see children stacking blocks and placing them in rows. They delight in stacking them and knocking them down. Later comes bridging, in which children place blocks across the tops of others. Before long, preschoolers are making enclosures and naming their structures. Older preschoolers can be seen building structures with greater attention to detail and incorporating dramatic play as they work together. These stages correlate to children's increasing cognitive ability to think abstractly. The blocks become symbols for other objects, such as a building or a tree. When children begin to pretend that one thing is something else, they are using the same cognitive processes they will use to understand that letters on a page are symbols for a word. Block play helps pave the way!

Developed by Caroline Pratt more than a century ago, wooden unit blocks work on a 1:2:4 ratio. When children place two of the smallest unit blocks together, they see that they equal the next size. This discovery helps children in understanding mathematical relationships. These hands-on experiences build the foundations of understanding part-to-whole and ultimately fractions.

INVITING CHILDREN TO ENGAGE IN BLOCK PLAY

Promote block play by providing a variety of blocks and by incorporating props such toy vehicles, animals, and people figurines. Through observation of children's play with blocks, you can determine which building materials children find engaging and when it is time to try something new. Store the blocks on low shelving so the children can choose which blocks they wish to use. Rotate props such as people and animal figurines to keep the children coming back to the block area. You can also set blocks out on mats or arrange them in simple vignettes to entice the children to explore.

BLOCK PLAY SUPPORTS LEARNING ACROSS THE DOMAINS

Block play can enhance the children's engagement in many ways. Through their explorations, children can develop language and literacy skills, fine and gross motor skills, social-emotional skills, science and math learning, and cognitive skills.

As they work, children have opportunities to name objects and have conversations. They develop vocabulary to describe what they are doing or want to do. By using signs and environmental print, they learn to recognize letters. As they label constructions or blueprints, they start with scribbling and can progress toward writing.

Block play supports both fine and gross motor development. Building helps develop eye-hand coordination when children place and fit blocks together. Children's spatial awareness of their bodies in relation to what they are building is heightened as they stretch and reach to build tall towers and large block arrangements.

Social-emotional development is supported through sharing and taking turns with preferred materials and through cooperating and negotiating while building constructions. Children develop self-regulatory skills when they experience emotions such as frustration when they cannot figure out how to make their constructions work.

Problem-solving when figuring out how to build what they are imagining helps with children's cognitive development. They discover mathematical relationships between blocks and develop scientific

concepts such gravity, angles, and speed when building ramps. The following is a list of blocks and props typically found in preschool classrooms.

- Wooden unit blocks
- Interlocking blocks
- Building blocks such as Lincoln Logs
- Animals, such as dinosaurs and those found on farms, in the sea, in the wild
- People
- Vehicles for land, water, and air travel
- Loose parts, such as cardboard and nature items
- Writing materials
- Masking tape
- Photos of structures

CREATE YOUR OWN BLOCKS

In addition to a sturdy set of unit blocks, you may want to create your own blocks to incorporate into the block area. You can make all sorts of blocks with images that are of interest to the children or that highlight curriculum concepts. You can create blocks that represent stone, brick, or wood. You can use the children's artwork to cover the block. (Just ask the child's permission first!) You can cover cardboard tubes with colored paper to inspire creative structures and emphasize specific colors. Cover them with contact paper or clear tape to make them more durable. You can create gradient color blocks by covering them with paint-sample cards. Create people blocks by using photos of the children in the classroom. Cover blocks with images from nature to emphasize and support science investigations.

Basic Blocks

Materials

Box: cardboard, tissue box, or other sturdy box

Newspaper

Colorful paper or fabric

Images (optional)

Maps or calendars (optional)

Clear packing tape or contact paper

1. Find a sturdy box.

2. Stuff it with wadded newspaper.

3. Wrap it in decorative paper or fabric, or decorate it with photos, images of architecture, maps, old calendars, wrapping paper, or children's artwork.

4. Cover with wide, clear tape or clear contact paper for durability.

Tubes

Materials

Cardboard tubes, such as paper-towel tubes or butcher-paper tubes

Colorful paper

Utility knife (adult use only)

Clear packing tape or clear contact paper

1. Cut the tubes into a variety of lengths. Shorter tubes will hold more weight, but longer tubes make great tunnels for toy vehicles. The children will love discovering this!

2. Cover each tube with colorful paper.

3. Cover the tubes with clear packing tape or contact paper for durability.

4. Encourage the children to explore ways to use the tubes in the block center.

BLOCKS ARE SUPER TOYS

For many years, educators and researchers have been interested in the ways in which children engage with blocks. They have discovered that blocks have the power to greatly enhance children's development. In a study that explored children's free play with sixty-four different classroom materials, blocks were found to score the highest on all of the measures, including creative expression, problem solving, social interactions, and language use. These findings led the researchers to call blocks *super toys* (Trawick-Smith, Russell, and Swaminathan, 2011).

Translucent Blocks

Materials

Wooden stacking-game pieces
Hot-glue gun (adult use only)
Colorful plastic dividers or folders
Scissors

1. Use hot glue to make frames using wooden stacking game pieces.

2. Cut squares from plastic dividers or folders to fit the wooden frames.

3. Glue a divider to one side of a frame, then sandwich another frame on top.

4. For added durability, squeeze wood glue into all seams.

CREATE ALTERNATIVE BLOCKS

Many common materials can be turned into blocks that will promote creativity in children's play. For example, coffee cans or egg cartons can become a set of large blocks. Children will delight in using these nontraditional building materials. Try incorporating some of the following materials into your block area.

- Large sponges
- Dominos
- Coffee cans (make sure any sharp edges are covered with duct tape)
- Plastic butter or yogurt tubs

- Cereal boxes
- Food boxes and containers
- Egg cartons
- Pool noodles

MATERIALS IN ACTION—BALANCING

Josie and Malik discover a bucket of pool-noodle blocks on the shelf in the block area. They dump the bucket on the floor and begin making stacks. As their towers get taller, they adjust their actions and become more deliberate in their placements. In their conversation, they discuss how tall their towers are, how hard it is to make them tall, and whose is tallest. Josie observes that you have to be really careful when the stack is tall or it will fall. She urges Malik to be careful so that his tower can get taller.

COLLECT MATERIALS TO USE WITH BLOCKS

To inspire creative play with blocks, teachers can collect a variety of materials that children can transport, line up, take apart, put together, and reuse in a multitude of open-ended ways. Simon Nicholson is credited with coining the term *loose parts* to describe such a collection of materials. It was his belief that children's interactions with open-ended materials would lead to greater creativity and problem-solving.

The following is just a partial list of the loose parts that could be added to the block center to enhance open-ended play:

- Cardboard boxes
- Cardboard tubes
- Pieces of cardboard
- Ice-pop or craft sticks
- Plastic cups
- Balls in a variety of sizes
- Fabric scraps

- Styrofoam
- Carpet scraps
- Linoleum scraps
- PVC pipe
- Dryer hoses
- Sponges
- Pool noodles

Mani and Reuben are having an intense discussion about who has more mini tree cookies. Both boys have a pile in front of them that they are guarding with their hands while they try to grab more. Mani insists that he has more. Reuben emphatically says, "No, I have more." Dara, who has been watching the struggle for a few moments, interjects, "You both have a lot, but maybe Mani has more. Yeah, Mani has more." Reuben again insists that he has more. Dara suggests that Mani should give Reuben some of his tree cookies so that they will have the same amount. Mani agrees, and the play continues.

- Flower pots
- Wooden planks
- Foam hair curlers
- Packing material
- Corks
- Pompoms
- Marbles
- Tin cans
- Thread spools
- Tree cookies

- Twigs, sticks, and branches
- Bark
- Leaves
- Driftwood
- Seed pods
- Acorns
- Logs
- Pebbles
- Rocks
- Pinecones

CREATE HOUSES AND STRUCTURES

To promote dramatic play and provide opportunities for problem solving, teachers can add houses, buildings, and other structures to the block area. You can construct simple structures out of cardboard, shoe boxes, coffee cans, or cardboard tubes. You and the children can paint or decorate them in any way you wish.

Chapter 2: Blocks and Props

Shoe-Box Barn

Materials

Scissors

Glue

Paint

Construction paper

Shoe box with lid

Toy animals, people, and vehicles

1. Cut windows into the sides of the shoe box.

2. Cut a barn door into one end of the shoe box.

3. Decorate the box and lid any way you wish to represent a barn.

4. Add toy animals, people, and vehicles.

Horse Corral

Materials

Cardboard box

Utility knife (adult use only)

Paint or construction paper and glue

1. Cut the sides of a cardboard box to resemble a fence.

2. Paint or decorate it, and add it to the shoe-box barn if you wish.

MATERIALS IN ACTION—MAKING PATTERNS

Taylor was delighted to find the bucket of loose parts her teacher had recently added to the block center of their classroom. She spent a large portion of the morning free-choice time exploring the various ceramic tiles, glass beads, and small tree cookies. Most of this time was devoted to sorting, but gradually she began to place the pieces in interesting patterns. At one point, she made a long line of alternating pieces. Her teacher noticed that she had created an AB pattern.

Craft-Stick Fence

Materials

4 craft sticks for each section of fence
Scissors
Hot-glue gun (adult use only)
Adhesive Velcro tape

1. Cut one stick in half.

2. Hot glue three craft sticks onto the two halves to create a fence section.

3. Repeat until you have made the number of fence sections you want.

4. Add adhesive Velcro tape to the fence ends so that they will stick together. To make the Velcro last longer, you may wish to hot glue the strips onto the fence sections.

Shoe-Box Car Wash

Materials

Felt	Paper-towel tubes
Scissors	Cardboard
Hot-glue gun	Craft sticks
(adult use only)	Shoe box with lid

1. Cut strips of felt to make fringe. The strips should fit around the circumference of a paper-towel tube.

2. Cut a paper-towel tube in half, and hot glue the fringe in rows around the cardboard tubes to create the rotating brushes.

3. Cut out two circles from a piece of cardboard. They should be larger than the opening in the paper-towel tubes.

4. Cut a 1/2-inch slit into the center of each cardboard circle, and insert a craft stick. Hot glue each craft stick into each cardboard circle.

5. Hot glue each circle onto the top of a tube.

6. Cut two holes into the shoe-box lid. Fit a craft stick through each hole.

7. Cut an opening into the side of the shoe box. Decorate the box if you wish.

8. Glue fringe onto the shoe-box lid to hang over the opening and act as the washing strips of the car wash.

9. Put the lid onto the shoe box.

10. Children can spin the craft-stick handles to rotate the brushes when pretending to wash cars.

Cardboard Parking Garage

Materials

Lid from copy-paper box or shoe box
Cardboard
Gray or black construction paper
Yellow or white paint pen
Scissors
Glue
2 paper-towel tubes
Construction paper

1. Cut two openings on either end of the copy-paper or shoe-box lid.

2. Line the box lid with gray or black construction paper. Glue it down to secure it.

3. Draw lines to indicate parking spaces.

4. Cut a piece of cardboard to the same size as the lid. Cover it with gray or black construction paper, and draw on parking spaces.

5. Cut the paper-towel tubes in half. Cover them with construction paper.

6. Stand the paper-towel tubes vertically on the corners of the cardboard. Glue each half of paper-towel tube onto a corner of the cardboard.

7. Glue the lid onto the tops of the paper-towel tubes.

Variation: Leave the paper-towel tubes unglued for children to construct in the manner they choose.

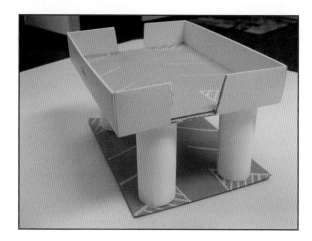

Cardboard-Box Doghouse

Materials

Shoe box or cardboard box
Utility knife (adult use only)
Construction paper and glue, or paint
Stuffed animal

1. Cut an opening into the end of the box, large enough to fit a stuffed animal through.

2. Decorate the box.

3. Turn the box over, and place the stuffed animal inside.

The manner in which children use materials can have an influence on their social and emotional development. Erik Erikson (1963) theorized that children often use toys in ways that could promote their social and emotional development as well as meet some of their psychological needs. For example, a child playing with the figurines in a dollhouse might be recreating family dynamics in a way that puts the child in a position of power at a time when the child feels powerless. Erikson believed that, while adults are able to talk out their emotional struggles, children needed to play out theirs. Toys and materials that teachers offer children can contribute to their ability to do so.

CREATE VEHICLES AND SIGNS

Vehicles are a well-loved prop in the block area. Add traffic signs to introduce literacy concepts into the children's play.

Craft-Stick Traffic Signs

Materials

Craft sticks

Hot-glue gun
  (adult use only)

Images of traffic signs

Plastic bottle or
  food-pouch caps

Clear packing tape

1. Find free images of traffic signs on the Internet. Print them and cut them out. Alternatively, you can create your own.

2. Cover the signs with clear packing tape for durability.

3. Glue them onto the ends of craft sticks.

4. Insert the other end of a craft stick into a bottle cap. You may have to cut a hole into the lid to make the craft stick secure.

5. Hot glue the stick onto the cap.

Cardboard-Tube Traffic Signs

Materials

Paper-towel tubes
Construction paper
Aluminum foil
Glue
Scissors
Images of traffic signs
Clear packing tape

1. Find free images of traffic signs on the Internet. Print them and cut them out. Alternatively, you can create your own.

2. Cut the paper-towel tubes in half.

3. Cover the tubes with construction paper.

4. Cut out a sign post from construction paper or aluminum foil.

5. Glue the sign post onto the decorated tube.

6. Glue on a traffic sign.

7. Cover with clear packing tape for durability.

Clothespin Traffic Signs

Materials

Clothespins
Black permanent marker or paint
Hot-glue gun (adult use only)
Images of traffic signs
Clear packing tape

1. Find free images of traffic signs on the Internet. Print them and cut them out. Alternatively, you can create your own.

2. Cover each sign with clear packing tape for durability.

3. Completely cover the surfaces of the clothespins with a black permanent marker or paint.

4. Attach the signs to the clothespins.

LaToya's teacher eavesdrops as LaToya plays with the stuffed dogs and the doghouse in the block center. She talks to herself and the dogs as she plays alone: "Oh, you're so sad because you are all alone. You want a friend in your house. Here's a friend for you. He can be in your house. Now you will be happy 'cause he's your friend. He's your friend." LaToya continues playing with the dogs. Her words indicate that she is beginning to understand empathy and is able to take another's perspective.

Cardboard Canoe

Materials

Paper-towel tube
Brown construction paper
Scissors
Glue
Brown permanent marker
Cardboard

1. Cut a paper-towel tube to the length you want.

2. Cut the tube lengthwise on one side.

3. Flatten the tube. Glue each end of the tube closed.

4. Cover the tube with brown construction paper, and trim the paper to fit. Glue on the construction paper.

5. Decorate the canoe with the marker.

6. Open the center of the tube slightly to create the look of a canoe.

7. Cut oars from the cardboard.

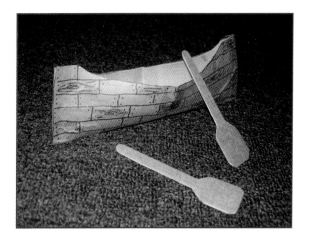

Cardboard Vehicles

Materials

Cardboard or recycled boxes

Plastic bottles (optional)

Straws

Scissors

Hot-glue gun (adult use only)

Food-pouch lids

Construction paper or free images of vehicles

1. Download and print free images of vehicles from the Internet.

2. Glue the images onto cardboard or pieces cut from recycled boxes.

3. Trim around the edges to create a vehicle shape. Alternatively, you can just cut out a vehicle shape and glue it to cardboard. Trim the paper to fit the shape.

4. Cut two holes in the vehicles at the bottom of the shape. This is where the wheels will go.

5. Cut a strong straw to 1-inch lengths.

6. Hot glue one end of each piece of straw into a food-pouch lid.

7. Thread the straws through the holes, and glue another lid to the end of the straw on the other side.

8. You can also make vehicles out of food boxes or plastic bottles using the same technique.

Variation: Cut out animal shapes and decorate them. Add wheels to create rolling animals.

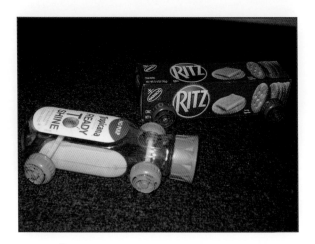

Some of the first words that children can "read" as their literacy awareness begins to grow are the signs and labels they see in their homes, in stores, and in their communities. For example, very young children can point out the logo of their neighborhood grocery store or a nearby fast-food restaurant. They recognize these particular words because of the colors, graphics, pictures, and shapes surrounding the print and because they see them so often. While children may not yet be able to name all of the letters in the sign or be able to sound out the words when written by hand, environmental print does help children begin to recognize that words are symbols and that they have meaning. Researchers have found that including environmental print in early childhood classrooms gives children the opportunity to feel successful "reading" at an early age and contributes to their literacy development (Giles and Tunks, 2010). Examples of environmental print include traffic signs, commercial signs, labels from household items, and food labels. Teachers can incorporate environmental print into their classrooms by adding food boxes, restaurant menus, and coupons to their dramatic-play props; by putting traffic signs or laminated store signs in the block area; by making books containing common signs, labels, and logos; or by making matching games, folder activities, and posters.

CREATE ROADWAYS AND TRACKS

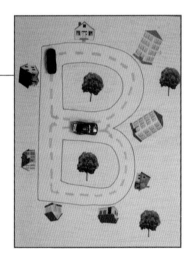

Roadways provide children with opportunities to use their fine-motor skills as they maneuver their vehicles around the twists and turns. You can introduce literacy learning opportunities by adding labeled roadways and maps to the block area.

Letter Map

Materials

Poster board

Markers and crayons

Images of houses, buildings, and trees

Toy vehicles

1. Draw a large "bubble" letter onto a piece of poster board.

2. Within the letter, draw dotted lines to indicate driving lanes.

3. Decorate the poster board, or let the children decorate it, to resemble a neighborhood or street.

4. Encourage the children to drive the toy vehicles on the letter map.

Ayako and Maddy pulled the box of traffic signs from the shelf and began placing them on the rug with the vehicles. As Ayako selected signs from the box, she "read" the signs aloud. When Maddy grabbed the speed limit sign, she said, "This one has numbers on it. Two and zero." Ayako replied, "That is twenty!"

Alphabet Parking Lot

Materials

Poster board
Pencil
Markers

Toy vehicles
Ruler

Variation: Instead of letters, write numerals in the parking spaces.

1. On a piece of poster board, mark twenty-six parking spaces with a pencil. Make sure each space is large enough to fit a toy vehicle.

2. Trace over the lines with marker. Within each parking space, write a letter of the alphabet.

3. Encourage the children to drive and park the toy vehicles in specific spaces and to name the letter in that space.

Cardboard Roadways

Materials

Cardboard pieces
Marker

Scissors

1. Cut cardboard into square and rectangular shapes.

2. On each piece, draw a road section with a dotted line in the center. You can create straight sections, curves, and intersections.

3. Encourage the children to put the pieces together in a variety of combinations to create roadways.

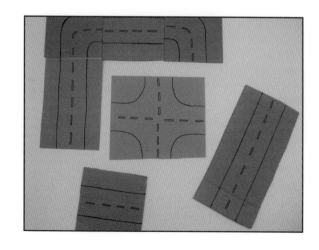

Felt Roadways

Materials

Black felt   Scissors

Glue   Toy vehicles

White tape

1. Cut felt into roadway sections. You can create straight sections, curves, and intersections.

2. Cut small strips out of the tape, and stick the bits onto the felt to create dotted lines.

3. Encourage the children to put the pieces together in a variety of combinations to create roadways for the toy vehicles.

CREATE TUNNELS AND BRIDGES

Young children enjoy opportunities to transport objects. Introducing tunnels and bridges into the block area will entice them to play.

Tube Bridge

Materials

Paper-towel tubes   Yellow construction

Cardboard   paper

Scissors   Glue

Black construction paper   Toy vehicles

1. Cut the paper-towel tubes in half. Cut slits in the sides of the tubes for the cardboard.

2. Cut the cardboard into a long rectangular strip.

3. Glue black construction paper onto the cardboard road, and cut it to fit.

4. Glue on small strips of yellow construction paper in a dotted line to create the lanes.

5. Fold the cardboard road at each end, approximately a third of the way up the cardboard. This will create a slope on either side.

6. Fit the cardboard road into the slits in the tubes. Glue the road in place.

7. Encourage the children to drive the toy vehicles over the bridge.

Hokulani and James are sitting on the floor in the block area running cars across the alphabet parking lot. Earlier in the morning, the classroom assistant teacher had been playing a game with James in which she would say a letter and then James would park his car in that space. Now, he is trying to teach Hokulani the game. She does not seem interested at first, but when he asks her to park in parking spot *H*, she perks up and says, "*H* is for Hokulani." Then she drives her car into that space. James replies, "*H* is for Hokulani. That's your name!"

Box Tunnel

Materials

Cardboard box	Glue
Scissors	Markers
Construction paper	

1. Remove the lid or top of a cardboard box. Save it for another use.

2. Cut *U*-shaped openings in opposite sides of the box.

3. Decorate the box with construction paper and markers.

4. Turn the box over to create a tunnel.

Half-Circle Tunnels

Materials

Cardboard insert of a packing-tape roll	Construction paper
	Cardboard
Utility knife (adult use only)	Toy vehicles

1. Cut the insert from a packing-tape roll in half.

2. Cut a strip of cardboard to the width of the interior of the packing-tape halves.

3. Cover the cardboard with construction paper to make it resemble a road.

4. Set the tunnels across the road.

5. Encourage the children to drive the toy vehicles through the tunnels.

Canister Tunnel

Materials

Oatmeal canister	Construction paper
Scissors or utility knife	(optional)
(adult use only)	Glue (optional)
Wooden blocks	Markers (optional)

1. Remove the lid, and cut the bottom off an oatmeal canister.

2. If desired, decorate the canister.

3. Set up the wooden blocks to create a road, and set some of the blocks inside the canister to create a road and tunnel.

4. Encourage the children to drive the vehicles through the tunnel.

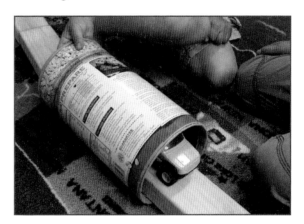

Mountain Tunnel and Pass

Materials

Cardboard	Scissors
Brown construction	Glue
paper	Hot-glue gun
White construction	(adult use only)
paper	Markers

1. Cut two pieces of cardboard to resemble a mountain.

2. Cover the mountains with glued-on construction paper, and decorate with markers.

3. Cut a U shape in the bottom of each mountain to create a tunnel opening in the mountain.

4. Cut a strip of cardboard to create a roadway.

5. Decorate the roadway with construction paper and markers.

6. Cut another, shorter strip of cardboard the same width as the roadway to create a tunnel.

7. Hot glue the tunnel strip in a U shape to the inside face of one side of the mountain. Hot glue the other side of the mountain to the other side of the tunnel.

8. Toward the top of the mountain, hot glue the roadway to each side to create a pass.

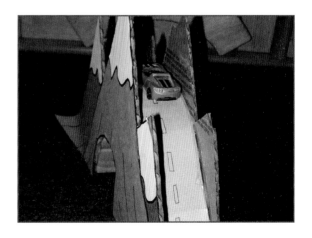

Sarah and Ekene enjoyed playing with the mountain tunnel after snack. In between having the cars drive over the mountain and the little people figurines walk over, Sarah told Ekene in great detail about her family's recent trip to Colorado. Ekene asked lots of questions and added his own thoughts and ideas about mountain roads. Their teacher noticed the growing friendship between the two classmates and the depth of their conversation.

CREATE LANDSCAPES

As children create dramatic-play scenarios in their block play, inspire them by including natural materials such as rocks and sticks as well as teacher-made landscape materials.

Cork Trees

Materials

Artificial evergreen garland	Scissors
Hot-glue gun (adult use only)	Corks

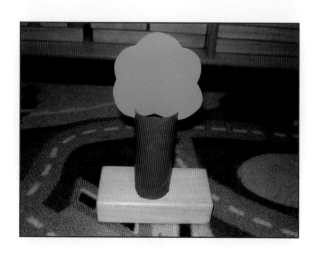

1. Cut pieces, which resemble trees, off the garland.

2. Stick each garland piece into the narrow end of a cork.

3. Hot glue the pieces in place.

Cardboard-Tube Trees

Materials

Paper-towel tube

Scissors

Green craft foam or poster board

Brown acrylic craft paint

Hot-glue gun (adult use only)

Styrofoam ball

1. Cut the paper-towel tube in half.

2. Paint it, if desired, to resemble a tree trunk.

3. Cut a leafy treetop out of the green craft foam or poster board.

4. Cut slits on either side of the paper-towel tube at one end.

5. Slide the treetop into the slits and secure with hot glue, or leave it unglued for children to construct.

Variation: Paint a Styrofoam ball green, and attach it to the top of a paper-towel tube tree trunk.

Cardboard Tree

Materials

Cardboard

Scissors

Green and brown paint

1. Cut two identical tree shapes out of a piece of cardboard.

2. Paint or decorate as desired.

3. Cut a slit in the bottom of one tree piece, and cut a slit in the top of the other tree piece.

4. Slide the two pieces together to create a standalone tree.

Habib was attracted to the two clothespin trees that he found in the block center. He placed the trees next to a stack of blocks. As his teacher passed by, he told her that he needed more trees. After a brief brainstorming session, the problem was solved when Habib decided to make more trees. The teacher pulled more clothespins from the storage closet, and Habib found some cardboard scraps in the collage bucket on the art shelf. Later, he proudly showed his teacher the six new trees he had made.

Felt Lake

Materials

Piece of blue felt (or blue paper or blue plastic tablecloth)

Small stones, shells, wood pieces

Scissors

Toy boats

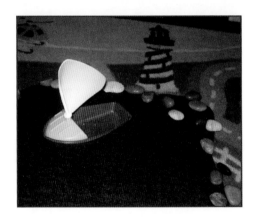

1. Cut out an amorphous shape from the felt.

2. Lay the felt on the floor in the block area, and surround it with small stones, shells, and wood to create a lake.

3. Set toy boats on the lake.

CREATE PEOPLE AND ANIMALS

Adding people and animals to the block areas increases children's language usage and story development. Children also get extremely excited by materials that include photographs of themselves and their friends.

Cardboard Story Characters

Materials

Paper-towel tubes

Construction paper

Markers

Scissors

Glue

1. Cut the paper-towel tubes in half.

2. Decorate the tubes with colored construction paper to create characters from the children's favorite stories. For example, use pink paper to create three little pigs. Then use gray or brown paper to create a wolf.

Cardboard Tube Animals

Materials

Paper-towel tubes   Markers
Scissors

1. Cut the paper-towel tubes in half.

2. On each piece, vertically draw an animal, such as a lion.

3. Color the animals with the markers.

4. Cut around the animal shapes, and cut all but about an inch or two of paper-towel tubes in the back. The animals will stand without support.

Clothespin Animals

Materials

Wooden clothespins   Card stock
Markers   Scissors
Free images of animals Googly eyes
  from the Internet, or Small pompoms
  draw your own   Glue
Felt   Clear packing tape

1. Print or draw images of animals. Or draw animal shapes on felt.

2. Cut out the images, and glue them onto card stock.

3. For durability, cover the images with clear packing tape.

4. Decorate the clothespins to resemble each animal's legs.

5. Clip the legs onto the animals.

6. If you wish, add googly eyes or pompom noses or tails.

Plastic Egg Animals

Materials

Plastic eggs	Googly eyes
Food-pouch lids	Glue
Construction paper	Hot-glue gun
Scissors	(adult use only)
Permanent markers	

1. Draw animal faces onto construction paper.

2. Cut out the faces and glue each onto a plastic egg. Glue on googly eyes.

3. Draw the animals' feet onto plastic food-pouch lids.

4. Hot glue the feet onto the eggs.

Cardboard Tube People

Materials

Photos of the children in the class	Scissors
	Glue
Paper-towel tubes	Clear packing tape
Construction paper	

1. Cut the paper-towel tubes in half.

2. Cover the tubes with construction paper.

3. Print and cut out photos of the children.

4. Use packing tape to secure a photo of a child to each tube.

Block Stand People

Materials

Photos of the children in the class	Scissors
	Clear packing tape
Clear contact paper or laminating machine	Wooden blocks

1. Print and cut out photos of the children.

2. Laminate the photos or cover them with clear contact paper, and trim around the edges.

3. Tape the photos to the wooden blocks.

Binder Clip People

Materials

Photos of the children in the class
Clear contact paper or laminating machine
Scissors
Binder clips

1. Print and cut out photos of the children. Leave a half-inch base at the bottom of each photo.

2. Laminate the photos or cover them with clear contact paper, and trim around the edges.

3. Clip a photo into each binder clip.

CREATE RAMPS

Ramps and tubes provide opportunities for children to explore concepts such as physics, gravity, angles, and speed. Through experimentation and problem solving, they will add to their understandings of how the world works.

Cardboard Tube

Materials

Wrapping-paper tube
Scissors
Marbles or small balls
Blocks

1. Cut the wrapping-paper tube in half lengthwise.

2. Encourage the children to prop one end of the tube on a stack of blocks, then roll a ball down the chute. They can experiment to find out how angle affects speed.

Several children are busy in the block center with the wood ramps and marbles. While stacking blocks and placing their ramps, they are encouraging each other to watch as they put their marbles in place. There is much excitement and squealing. Jon keeps insisting that they need to make it higher. He says, "When it's high, it goes so fast. Watch it go fast, fast, fast!" Iman helps him stack the blocks higher before putting the ramp back in place. "Hey, everybody! Watch this!" Jon yells, as he places three marbles at the top of the ramp before letting go. As they roll down, the other children clamor for a turn at his ramp.

PVC Pipe

Materials

PVC pipe	Blocks
PVC pipe cutter or handsaw (adult use only)	Marbles or small balls that will fit through the pipe

1. Cut the PVC pipe into a variety of lengths yourself, or ask to have them cut when purchasing the pipe at a home-improvement store.

2. Encourage the children to prop one end of a tube on a stack of blocks, then roll a ball down the chute. They can experiment to find out how angle affects speed.

Pool-Noodle Ramps

Materials

Pool noodle	Blocks
Scissors	Marbles or small balls

1. Cut the pool noodle in half lengthwise.

2. Encourage the children to prop one end on a stack of blocks, then roll a ball down the chute. They can experiment to find out how angle affects speed.

Wood Molding Ramps and Marble Run

Materials

Wood molding scraps

Handsaw (adult use only)

Sandpaper

Blocks

Marbles

1. Gather wood molding scraps. You might ask families to donate these from household projects, or you could ask a construction firm to donate.

2. Cut the scraps to a variety of lengths. Sand the ends to remove any splintery bits.

3. Encourage the children to prop one end on a stack of blocks, then roll a marble down the chute. They can experiment to find out how angle affects speed.

4. They can also create structures, such as a marble run.

COLLECT AND CREATE CONSTRUCTION INSPIRATIONS

Adding tools and other construction images to the block area increases opportunities for children to engage with math and literacy concepts in an open-ended and contextual manner. The following is a list of materials that could be added to the block center to enhance explorations.

- Measuring tapes
- Rulers
- Toy tools
- Real tools
- Clipboards
- Paper
- Writing utensils

- Hard hats
- Blueprints and building plans
- Photos of buildings, bridges, and other structures from around the world, glued onto cardboard and laminated
- Photos of construction sites and construction workers, glued onto cardboard and laminated

After noticing how much the children had engaged with some rulers he had placed in the block area, Mr. Mitchell decided to add a measuring tape. Tomás found it first and spent some time simply pulling the tape out and pushing the retracting mechanism over and over again. Next, he began stretching the tape across the top of the unit blocks by holding the cartridge in one hand and pulling the tape with his other hand. Eventually, Tomás discovered that he could hook the end of the tape on the edge of the block and then pull the tape measure. He moved on to "measure" the shelf and the table before Safiyah noticed what he was doing and wanted to have a turn.

Accordion Book of Building Ideas

Materials

Blocks

Digital camera

Poster board

Glue

Clear contact paper or laminating machine

Scissors

Clear packing tape

1. Create a variety of structures with wooden blocks.

2. Photograph each one, and enlarge and print the photos.

3. Glue each photo onto a piece of poster board.

4. Laminate or cover the photos with clear contact paper. Trim with scissors.

5. Connect each page of the accordion book to the next page with clear packing tape.

3 Dramatic-Play Materials

Naijeer and Annie could often be seen in the dramatic play area of the classroom pretending to be the mommy and daddy to their baby doll. One morning, they were very concerned that their baby was sick. Annie kept telling Naijeer that they had to get the baby to eat. She tried the trick of

pretending the spoon was an airplane and then pleaded, "Please, baby. You have to eat something! Oh, no, I think the baby is sick!" Naijeer joined in with the pleading before declaring, "That's it. You have to go to the doctor. You have to have a shot." Using a cell-phone prop, he called the doctor to "get a appointment," using a serious tone. They were still in the process of putting the baby in a carrier when it was time to clean up.

Dramatic-play scenarios like this one are common is preschool classrooms. Children enjoy playing together in pretend roles, both using the props around them and creating their own. Research continues to show the value and importance of this type of make-believe. When children engage in dramatic play, they learn how to cope with feelings, practice new vocabulary, and problem solve social situations.

Teachers can support children's dramatic play and learning by closely observing what interests them, making note of common themes in their play, and introducing them to new materials they can utilize. By collecting and creating materials over time, it is easy to enhance the classroom environment with relevant props. One way that teachers might do this is by creating prop boxes related to common themes such as a doctor's office or a bakery. By planning ahead, teachers can reduce their time spent finding the right props.

INVITING CHILDREN TO PARTICIPATE IN DRAMATIC PLAY

Teachers can invite children to play by creating scenes in the dramatic-play area, such as setting a table with a baby doll in a high chair or lining up the doctor's-kit instruments on a shelf. By paying close attention to the themes in children's dramatic play, teachers can decide when to add new materials that support the children's ideas and will know when to remove items that no longer seem to hold their interest. Teachers might also add items related to their curriculum as part of their regular planning. For example, a curriculum theme or project about transportation might lead a teacher to add props such as car keys or an infant car seat.

DRAMATIC PLAY WITH MATERIALS SUPPORTS LEARNING ACROSS DOMAINS

Dramatic play can support learning in and across the domains of language and literacy development; fine and gross motor development; social-emotional development; and science, math, and cognitive development.

Children develop their language and literacy skills by engaging in conversations with each other during pretend play. They have opportunities to use vocabulary specific to the props and themes of their play, helping them learn new words within a context. They can learn about everyday literacy concepts such as following a recipe and making grocery lists.

Fine motor development is supported through putting on dress-up clothes, fastening buttons and snaps, and zipping zippers. Children develop eye-hand coordination by pushing the buttons on a pretend phone. They learn to coordinate their actions, a gross motor skill, by setting the table while holding a baby doll.

Solving the conflicts that occur when multiple children are playing together for a purpose helps children learn to navigate social situations with peers. Pretending to have a birthday party or taking on roles and deciding who gets to play which role can require negotiation, patience, and communication. As they play, children develop the self-regulation skills that enable them to wait their turn for the stethoscope or share the food props. Through role play, children have opportunities to express real and pretend emotions and learn to recognize them in others.

Dramatic play can also support science, math, and cognitive development. Recalling the order of routines, such as getting dressed or cooking dinner, helps children learn sequence. They learn to think symbolically as they use a craft-stick thermometer to take the baby's temperature. They have opportunities to deepen their understanding of one-to-one correspondence by passing out one plate, one cup, and one utensil to each person at the table. The following are materials typically found in dramatic-play centers in preschool classrooms.

- Child-size furniture, such as tables, chairs, kitchen sink, stove, and baby bed
- Pretend food and dishes
- Baby dolls and accessories
- Dress-up clothes and shoes

- Real items, such as wicker baskets and suitcases
- Environmental print, such as empty food boxes, menus, cookbooks, and grocery lists
- Community-helper props, such as stethoscopes and firefighter helmets

COLLECT REAL MATERIALS FOR DRAMATIC PLAY

Children absolutely love using real objects in their play. They will often make a beeline to those items first, and teachers will see children showing a preference for those items. Researchers have found that not only do children play with realistic props longer, but they also use more language while playing with them as compared other materials (Doctoroff, 2001; McLoyd, 1986). This has led many early childhood teachers to incorporate more real items into their dramatic play centers. From dress-up clothes to housewares, these materials are easy to come by and will provide countless hours of play and learning.

Asking classroom parents to donate gently used clothing and other household goods when they clean out their closets is a good way to start. Garage sales, thrift stores, and dollar stores are also good resources that are relatively inexpensive. The following lists just some of the materials that you could put in your dramatic play area:

- Kitchen gadgets—real pots, pans, kitchen utensils, cookie sheets, spatulas, plastic ware, oven mitts
- Dress-up clothing—dresses, jackets, hats, clip-on ties, shoes and boots, scarves, slippers, suits or vests in larger children's or teenage sizes, sunglasses, purses, jewelry

- Containers—wicker baskets and trays, suitcases, backpacks, purses, wallets, tote bags, holiday tins, decorative boxes
- Appliances and electronics—old cell phones, telephones, cameras, keyboards, computer screen, clocks, watches

Safety Note: When using real appliances and electronics, be sure to remove the batteries and cut off the electrical cords.

Sandeep and Tristan are both wearing men's suit jackets. Tristan asks their teacher for help putting on a clip-on tie. He tells her they have to go to work. Sandeep has a baby doll in a carrier that he is carrying, and he tells Tristan to get his baby. Tristan finds another doll and carrier. He struggles to get the baby situated in the seat, so Sandeep helps him. They both walk around in their suits carrying the baby carriers. As they play, the teacher overhears some of their comments: "We've got to get to work . . . We can't be late . . . I will be back later . . . Don't cry . . . Let's pretend they fell asleep . . . I don't want to wake him up . . . I have to go to work now . . . It's time to go . . . I'm back!"

- Fabric—pillows, pillow cases, blankets, afghans, placemats, fabric scraps

- Home accessories—artificial flowers and plastic vases; cleaning supplies such as empty spray bottles, sponges, small hand brooms with dustpans, clothesline and clothespins

- Baby care—baby blankets, bath towels, car seat, bottles, toys, baby carriers, bassinets

CULTURAL LEARNING AND PLAY

The materials provided for young children can affect their cultural understandings of the world. Toys and materials might be thought of as representations of various cultures (Sutton-Smith, 1995), and when children engage with materials, they do so in cultural ways. As children imitate social and cultural practices in their play, they can be limited by the materials provided. When children have cultural props for dramatic play that represent their own and other cultures, their play is enhanced. For example, when teachers provide food and clothing props that represent the diversity of the children in their classroom, children have the opportunity to explore and understand the experiences of others.

CREATING MATERIALS FOR DRAMATIC PLAY

In the absence of real objects, you can make props for children to use in dramatic play. When a teacher creates a doghouse out of a box, the children will search to find a stuffed animal to sleep inside. If they find a sandwich made from craft foam on a table, that sandwich could end up in a wicker basket on its way to a picnic. While children are extremely capable of making their own props, teacher-made props can jump-start children's imaginations and enhance their creative dramatic play.

As you see children engaging in dramatic play, ideas of materials to include will often become apparent. Children's interest in pretend cooking, for example, might lead you to make more food props. After noticing their engagement with baby dolls, you could create a crib from a box to add to the dramatic-play center. To kick off a project on transportation, you might surprise the children with a train made from several boxes.

Paper-Plate Food

Materials
Paper plates
Magazines
Scissors
Glue

1. Let the children find photos of food in magazines.

2. Encourage them to cut out foods they like or foods they would like to try.

3. The children can glue the images onto paper plates and use these props in the dramatic-play center.

Craft Foam or Felt Sandwiches

Materials

Felt or craft foam in a variety of colors

Scissors

Marker

Pencil

1. Sketch sandwich ingredients on pieces of felt. You could make bread from tan felt, tomato from red, lunch meat from pink, lettuce from green, cheese from yellow, peanut butter from brown, and jelly from purple.

2. Cut out the shapes, and sketch details onto them with a marker, if you wish.

3. Place them in the play kitchen.

Felt Pasta

Materials

Tan felt

Cotton balls

Hot-glue gun (adult use only)

Scissors

Needle and thread (adult use only)

To make ravioli:

1. Cut two square shapes from the felt.

2. Hot glue three sides together and let dry.

3. Stuff the ravioli with cotton balls.

4. Seal the fourth side with hot glue.

To make bow-tie pasta:

1. Cut a rectangle from the felt.

2. Fold the piece lengthwise in an accordion pattern.

3. Crimp the center together and stitch it with needle and thread to hold it together.

Felt Egg Rolls

Materials

Paper-towel roll

Beige felt

Paper

Craft foam scraps

Scissors

Hot-glue gun (adult use only)

1. Cut the paper-towel roll in half.

2. Cover each half with beige felt and trim to fit.

3. Glue the felt in place.

4. Stuff the roll with wadded paper and scraps of craft foam to create the filling. Glue in place.

Natural Twine Noodles

Materials

Natural twine

Felt in a variety of colors

Scissors

Chopsticks

Take-out food containers

1. Cut natural twine to 8-inch lengths to create noodles.

2. Cut pieces of felt to represent vegetables, such as carrots, celery, corn, peppers, and mushrooms.

3. In a take-out container, put the noodles and vegetables, along with some chopsticks.

Felt Eggs

Materials

White felt	Glue
Yellow felt	6 plastic eggs
Scissors	Egg carton

1. Cut the white felt into the shape of a cooked egg white. Cut the yellow felt into a circle to represent the yolk.

2. Glue the two pieces together to create an egg.

3. Place each egg into a plastic egg, and put each egg in an egg carton.

Felt Fajitas

Materials

Beige felt	Scissors
Felt in a variety of colors	Plastic tortilla warmer

1. Cut a circle from the beige felt, approximately 8 inches in diameter, to create a tortilla.

2. Cut vegetables and toppings from the colored felt: green and red peppers, tomato slices, cheese, onion, and so on.

   Place the tortillas in the warmer. **Note:** You can purchase inexpensive tortilla warmers from a dollar store.

3. Place the toppings on a plate.

Felt Pizza

Materials

Beige or tan felt	Scissors
Felt in a variety of colors	

1. Cut out a large circle from the beige or tan felt.

2. Cut out toppings from the colored felt: pepperoni, cheese, peppers, onions, mushrooms, olives, tomatoes, sausage, spinach, and so on.

3. Let the children create their own pretend pizzas!

Sushi

Materials

Craft foam

Hot-glue gun (adult use only)

Black felt

Green felt

White shelf liner

Recycled sushi trays

To make seaweed-wrapped sushi:

1. Cut 1-inch squares from craft foam, and fringe the opposite sides to create the fish or vegetable stuffing.

2. Roll the squares up and secure with hot glue.

3. Cut black felt into 1-inch-wide strips. Wrap a black strip around the filling. Secure with hot glue.

4. Cut white shelf liner into strips.

5. Wrap white shelf liner around stuffing multiple times to create rice and secure with hot glue.

6. Wrap with green felt and secure with hot glue to imitate seaweed.

   Optional: Spread hot glue across ends to make more durable.

7. Add sushi trays from the recycling bin.

Sponge Cake

Materials

Sponges

Acrylic paint

Paintbrushes

Puffy paint

Red pompom

Hot-glue gun (adult use only)

Scissors or craft knife (adult use only)

1. Cut the sponge into a triangular or round shape.

2. Paint the top with acrylic paint to create icing.

3. Add sprinkles using puffy paint.

4. Glue a red pompom cherry on top.

Felt Cinnamon Roll

Materials

Brown or purple felt

Tan felt

Hot-glue gun (adult use only)

White puffy paint

1. Cut the tan felt into a 2″ × 12″) rectangle.

2. Fold it in half, and roll it from one end to create a cinnamon roll. Glue the end in place.

3. Top the roll with white puffy-paint icing.

4. Cut out raisins from the brown or purple felt. Glue these on top of the roll.

Cardboard Cookies

Materials

Cardboard   Puffy paint

Scissors   Glue

Felt or craft foam

1. Cut out circles from the cardboard.

2. Glue on a piece of felt or craft foam as the icing.

3. Add puffy-paint sprinkles.

Cardboard Wafer Cookies

Materials

Cardboard   Glue

Scissors   Brown marker

Sponges

1. Cut cardboard into rectangles.

2. Cut the sponges to the same size as the rectangles.

3. Glue two rectangles onto each sponge: one on the top and one on the bottom.

4. Draw details onto the cardboard cookies.

Bonita is playing with the felt sandwich pieces. She tells Midori that she is going to make her a sandwich for lunch. She says, "First you take the bread. Then you put the cheese on it. It's the kind that has the holes in it. Then you put some bologna. Next is some other kind of meat—I don't know what it is. Now some lettuce. Do you like lettuce?" Midori nods. Bonita continues, "Do you like tomatoes? I don't like tomatoes, but I will put them on your sandwich if you like them." Midori nods again. "Okay. I gave you two tomatoes. And last is the bread. There you go. There's your sandwich. Do you like it?"

CREATE DRAMATIC-PLAY PROPS FROM BOXES

Just adding cardboard boxes to the dramatic-play area will spark children's imaginations to create their own props. Teachers can also make props from boxes that will spur dramatic play.

Washing Machine

Materials

Cardboard

Large cardboard box

Small plastic basket

Markers

Paint

Packing tape or duct tape

Scissors or box cutter (adult use only)

1. Tape the large box closed.

2. On the top of the box, set the basket upside down, and trace around it with a marker.

3. Cut out the circle one quarter inch smaller than the outline, so the basket has a place to rest, and drop the basket into the hole to create a washer bin.

4. Tape a piece of cardboard to the back top edge of the box to create a lid over the washer bin.

5. Cut a rectangle from a piece of cardboard. Decorate it with dials using the markers or paint to create a control panel.

6. Tape the control panel to the top, back side of the washer.

Cardboard Cradle

Materials

Rectangular box large enough to fit a baby doll

Cardboard

Marker

Scissors or box cutter (adult use only)

Hot-glue gun (adult use only)

Baby doll bedding

Baby doll

1. Trace two end pieces onto the cardboard. The bottoms of the end pieces should be curved so that the cradle can be rocked. The pieces should be large enough to extend beyond the top and bottom of the rectangular cardboard box.

2. Cut out the two end pieces for the cradle from the cardboard.

3. Glue the end pieces onto the ends of the rectangular box. Decorate as desired.

4. Place the bedding into the box, along with a baby doll.

Mailbox

Materials

Cardboard box

Pieces of cardboard

Blue butcher paper

Glue

Markers or paint

Clear packing tape

White paper

1. Cut two half circles from cardboard so that the diameter matches the size of the side of the box. Secure the half circles to the top sides of the box with clear packing tape.

2. Cut a rectangle from cardboard that fits the curve. Secure with hot glue or tape. This will form the top of the mailbox.

3. Cut a door in the curved cardboard. Cover with blue butcher paper, and secure the paper with tape or glue.

4. Make a sign to attach to the front of the mailbox with glue.

Train

Materials

3 large cardboard boxes	Oatmeal canisters
Butcher paper in 3 colors	Box cutter (adult use only)
Black construction paper	2 metal pie tins
Plastic bottle caps or food-pouch caps	Hot-glue gun (adult use only)
Markers	Paint
Painter's tape	Paintbrushes
Cardboard tubes	Small step stool

To make the engine:

1. Cover a large box in butcher paper.

2. On the front, attach a piece of cardboard cut to resemble a cowcatcher.

3. Cut two rectangular pieces of cardboard, one larger than the other. Roll them into circular shapes. Attach the larger circle to the front of the engine.

4. Inside the larger circle, attach the smaller circle to resemble a headlight.

5. Decorate the headlight and cowcatcher with painter's tape, paint, and butcher paper.

6. Cut out circles from black construction paper to resemble wheels. On each side of the engine, attach the wheels.

7. Decorate the sides of the engine with painter's tape and other decorations as you see fit.

8. Cut a cardboard tube to approximately 12 inches in length.

9. Cover it with butcher paper, and attach the tube to the top of the engine.

10. Glue the metal pie tins together, face-to-face, and glue those onto the top of the tube to resemble a smokestack.

11. Remove the lid, and cut the bottom off of an oatmeal canister.

12. Cover it with butcher paper, and attach it to the top of the engine behind the first smokestack.

13. Inside the engine, create a control panel by hot gluing plastic bottle caps or food-pouch caps onto the inside of the box. Draw on dials and other instruments.

To make a passenger car:

1. Cut the top off a large cardboard box.

2. On one side of the box, cut the side in half down the center. Then cut along the bottom of one half to create a door. Cut approximately 6 inches off the top of the door to create a window effect.

3. Cover the entire box with butcher paper.

4. Decorate the sides of the passenger car with painter's tape.

5. Cut out circles from construction paper to resemble wheels. Add two wheels on either side of the box.

6. Add a small bench inside the car as seating.

To make a caboose:

1. Cut the top off a large cardboard box.

2. At one corner, cut down from the top to the bottom and halfway along the base to create a door.

3. Cover the entire box with butcher paper.

4. Cut out circles from construction paper to resemble wheels. Add wheels on either side of the box.

5. Decorate the car with painter's tape and other decorations as desired.

Bakery Stand

Materials

Large cardboard box	Packing tape
4–6 shoe boxes or snack boxes, all the same type	Cardboard
	4 cardboard tubes
	Butcher paper
Scissors or box cutter (adult use only)	Glue

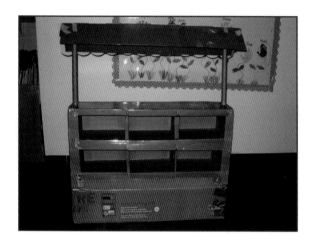

1. Collect shoe boxes or snack boxes of the same type.

2. Cut rectangular holes in the larger box.

MATERIALS IN ACTION—COUNTING

When the preschoolers come in from outside, they find near the writing center a mailbox made from a cardboard box. Paper, envelopes, junk mail, and stamps are spread out on the table with containers of writing utensils. Immediately, several children get excited about the idea of mailing letters and begin scribbling on paper and stuffing envelopes. Zach says he is going to mail a letter to his uncle in Virginia. Bhamini and Sarah seem more interested in just putting the envelopes in the mailbox. The assistant teacher notices their stack and says, "Wow! That is a lot of letters you are mailing. I wonder how many there are." Sarah decides to count them as she puts them in the mailbox. Bhamini joins in. After they get to seven, Bhamini says, "Let's get more! Let's mail ten letters!"

3. Create cubby holes inside the large box by folding the flaps of the snack boxes together and securing with strong tape.

4. Create an awning by firmly taping four cardboard tubes vertically on each corner of the stand.

5. Tape a piece of cardboard on top to create the top of the awning.

6. Decorate the stand with butcher paper.

CREATING MATERIALS FOR ROLE PLAY

Simple accessories such as hats and tutus inspire more creative dramatic play.

Craft Foam and Straws Lei

Materials
Craft foam in a variety of colors
Scissors
Green plastic straws
String or yarn
Masking tape

1. Cut out flower shapes from the craft foam. Use scissors to poke a small hole into the center of each flower.

2. Cut a length of string or yarn. Put a bit of masking tape around one end to make stringing easier.

3. Cut the straws into 2-inch lengths.

4. Add craft-foam flowers and straw pieces onto the string, alternating flowers and straws, until the string is filled. Leave a little room at the ends to tie off the string.

5. Tie a knot in the string to create a lei.

Tulle Tutu

Materials

Elastic headband or length of elastic tape
Tulle or ribbon in a variety of colors

1. Use an elastic headband purchased from a dollar store, or cut a length of elastic tape large enough to fit comfortably around a child's waist. Sew or tie the elastic tape together to create a loop.

2. Cut strips of tulle or ribbon.

3. Tie the strips onto the elastic.

Pirate Hat

Materials

Foam cowboy hat
Hot-glue gun (adult use only)
Craft feather

1. Fold up three parts of the rim of the hat to create a tricornered hat.

2. Hot glue the sides to the crown of the hat.

3. Hot glue a feather on the hat.

Jet Pack

Materials

2 plastic soda bottles or 2 cardboard tubes
Silver spray paint or butcher paper (any color)
Silver duct tape or string
Red, yellow, and orange paper streamers
   or fabric
Hot-glue gun (adult use only)

1. Away from the children in a well-ventilated area, spray-paint the bottles silver. If using cardboard tubes, you can cover them with colored paper.

2. Duct tape the bottles or tubes together.

3. Create shoulder straps by folding strips of duct tape in half or by cutting lengths of string and attaching them to the jet pack with hot glue. Make sure that the shoulder straps are large enough to comfortably slide over a child's shoulders.

4. At the bottom of the jet pack, add "flames" made from strips of colored paper or fabric.

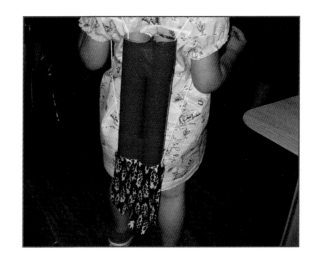

T. rex Feet

Materials
Green flip-flops
Scissors

1. Purchase a pair of green flip-flops from a thrift or dollar store.

2. Cut the edges of the shoes to create a reptilian footprint, making sure not to cut the straps.

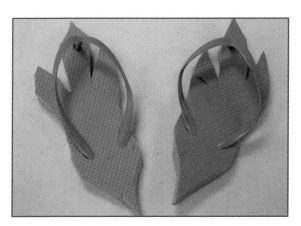

Dinosaur Hat

Materials
Green craft foam	Hot-glue gun
White felt	(adult use only)
Black felt	Scissors
Green baseball cap	

1. Purchase a green baseball cap from a thrift or dollar store.

2. Cut triangles from the craft foam.

3. Glue the triangles onto the top of the hat to create a crest.

4. Cut out eyes from the white felt, and glue those onto the front of the hat. Add black felt pupils to complete the eyes.

5. Cut out triangles from the white felt to create teeth.

6. Glue the teeth onto the underside of the brim.

Dinosaur Tail

Materials

Green felt

Yellow craft foam

Scissors

Cotton balls or batting

Hot-glue gun

    (adult use only)

1. Cut the green felt into a large triangle.

2. Cut out triangles from the yellow craft foam.

3. Fold the large green felt triangle in half.

4. Hot glue the yellow foam triangles along the inside edge of the long side of the felt triangle.

5. Hot glue the long side of the triangle to seal it.

6. Stuff the tail with cotton, and hot glue the opening to seal it.

7. Cut two pieces of felt into long strips, and attach these to the tail.

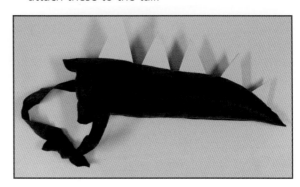

Dinosaur Helmet

Materials

Green plastic construction helmet

Green craft foam or construction paper

Masking or packing tape

Scissors

1. Purchase a plastic construction helmet from a thrift or dollar store. If you can't find green, any color will do.

2. Cut triangles from the craft foam or construction paper.

3. Tape the triangles onto the top of the helmet to create a crest.

Dinosaur Claws

Materials

Work gloves

Green craft foam

Scissors

Hot-glue gun

    (adult use only)

1. Cut the fingertips off the work gloves.

2. Cut out claw shapes from the craft foam.

3. Hot glue the claws onto the insides of the glove fingertips.

4. Cut out small spikes from the craft foam, and glue these onto the outside of the gloves.

Fox Ears

Materials

Plastic headband	Hot-glue gun
Brown craft foam	(adult use only)
Tan or pink craft foam	Scissors

1. Purchase a plastic headband from a thrift or dollar store.

2. Fold the brown craft foam in half, and cut an ear shape on the fold so that, when opened, you have mirror images.

3. Cut two small slits along the fold for the headband to slide through.

4. Hot glue both sides of the ear together, starting from the top and leaving the area next to fold unglued.

5. Cut out two smaller triangles from the tan or pink craft foam.

6. Glue these onto the fox ear.

7. Repeat these steps for the other ear.

8. Slide the ears onto the plastic headband. Secure with hot glue if necessary.

MATERIALS IN ACTION—SOCIAL PROBLEM SOLVING

Josie and Salvador both want to wear the cowboy boots they have found in the dress-up box. They stand together, each holding a boot and telling each other that they want to wear them first. Josie puts her boot on and tries to pull the other one out of Salvador's hands, but he will not let go. He sits down on the floor looking very unhappy. Bethany has been watching the quarrel and wants to help. She asks Salvador if Josie can wear them first and then he can have a turn. Salvador shakes his head no. Bethany then turns to Josie and asks if Salvador can wear them first. Josie reluctantly agrees. She pulls off the boot and tosses it toward Salvador, who grabs it and puts it on. Josie reminds Salvador that she gets a turn next.

Butterfly Wings

Materials

Poster board   Markers and crayons
Hole punch   Scissors
Ribbon

1. Trace butterfly wings onto poster board.

2. Cut out the shape, and let the children decorate the wings.

3. Punch two holes at the top of the wings.

4. Cut two lengths of ribbon long enough to fit comfortably over a child's shoulders.

5. Thread the two ribbons through the holes, knotting the ribbons firmly.

6. Punch two holes at the bottom of the wings.

7. Thread the other ends of the ribbons through the holes and knot them firmly.

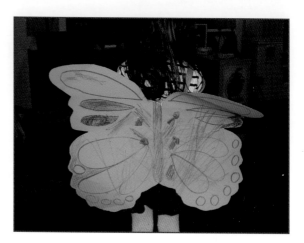

CREATE COSTUMES

When children put on costumes and pretend to be characters, they begin to see from the perspective of others. What would a police officer say and do? How does a baker behave? The costume helps them carry the idea of the role in their minds and sustains dramatic play.

Purchase T-shirts from a thrift or dollar store. Attach decorations made from felt or craft foam with hot glue. These can be gently hand washed and allowed to air dry.

Doctor

Materials

White shirt
Fabric paint

1. Write *Doctor* on one side of the front of a white shirt.

2. Draw on a red cross or other emblem to indicate a medical professional.

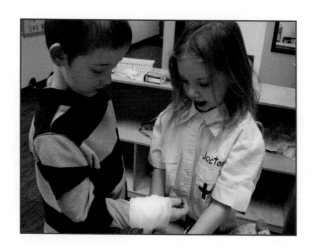

Sheriff's Deputy

Materials

Brown T-shirt

Tan felt

Black felt

Yellow felt

Fabric paint

Hot-glue gun
    (adult use only)

Buttons (optional)

Needle and thread (optional,
    adult use only)

1. Cut a tie shape from the tan felt, and glue it onto the front center of the T-shirt.

2. From the black felt, cut out pockets and glue these onto the front of the shirt.

3. Cut out sheriff stars from the yellow felt. Glue these onto the front and sleeves of the shirt.

4. Write *Sheriff* or *Deputy* on the sleeves.

5. If you like, add details such as buttons, and create a shield from felt to glue onto one sleeve.

MATERIALS IN ACTION—ROLE PLAY

Eva puts on the firefighter T-shirt costume and grabs a short length of hose that has been added as a prop for firefighter play. She begins yelling, "Oh, no! That house is on fire! Let's get everybody out!" She runs over to the block area where several children are building and knocks over part of their structure in the process. They are not happy and let her know. David, who had been with the builders, decides to join Eva, and they both spread the news of the fire around the room. Most of the other children are busy doing other activities so it takes a while to find someone who responds in kind. Aaron, who had been washing his hands, yells out, "The fire's over here! Help! Call 9-1-1!" Eva and David run over to him and pretend to spray water on a fire that has sprung up in the middle of the room. Eva keeps pointing to random areas, and all three children work to fight the fires.

Firefighter

Materials

Red T-shirt

Scissors

Yellow felt

White felt

Red felt

Hot-glue gun (adult use only)

Red marker

1. Cut the T-shirt down the front center to create a jacket.

2. Add Velcro strips along the opening to create a closable jacket.

3. Cut out strips from the yellow felt to create a belt and sleeve decorations. Glue these in place.

4. From the white felt, cut out clasp shapes, and glue these down one side of the jacket opening.

5. Cut out pockets from the red felt, and glue these on the front of the shirt.

6. If you like, create a shield decoration on one side of the front of the shirt.

Postal Worker

Materials

Blue T-shirt

Blue visor

Scissors

Adhesive Velcro tape

Hot-glue gun (adult use only)

Blue or white felt

Markers

Fabric paint

Tip: You can laminate different logos or badges and add Velcro to the backs to create interchangeable badges for different costumes.

1. Cut the T-shirt down the front center.

2. Add Velcro strips along the opening to create a closable jacket.

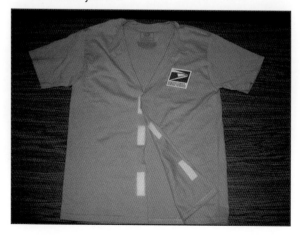

3. If desired, add a logo or name badge made from blue or white felt and drawn with markers.

4. Decorate the visor with fabric paint.

Chef

Materials

White T-shirt

Black fabric paint or permanent marker

White poster board

Scissors

White tissue paper

Glue

1. Decorate the T-shirt with a drawn-on pocket with utensils in it.

2. Draw or paint on buttons and shirt details.

3. For the toque, or chef's hat, cut a strip of poster board and glue it to create a circle that will fit on a child's head.

4. Glue tissue paper to the inside of the circle to create the top of the hat.

Stick Horse

Materials

Decorative tube sock

Cotton batting

Felt

Hot-glue gun (adult use only)

Cardboard

Scissors

Yarn

Long cardboard tube

Ribbon

Buttons (optional)

1. Stuff a dollar-store sock with cotton batting.

2. For each ear, cut pieces from felt. Cut out a smaller piece of cardboard, and hot glue it onto the felt ear for stability. Leave a little at the bottom; this will provide a flap that can be glued to the sock.

3. Cut eyes and nostrils from felt, and attach them with hot glue.

4. Cut yarn into 8-inch lengths, and tie them into bundles for the mane.

5. Glue on the ears.

6. Attach one bundle of yarn in front of the ears to hide the flap and then continue with the other bundle behind the ears.

7. Use a sturdy cardboard tube for the stick. Slide the tube into the sock, ensuring that it reaches

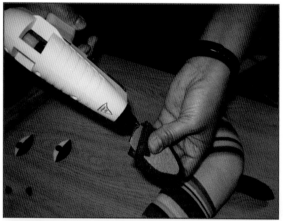

the heel of the sock, which would be the top of the head.

8. Secure the opening of the sock to the tube with hot glue.

9. Attach ribbon with hot glue to create reins. Add a decorative button to each side, if you wish.

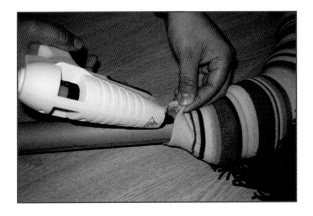

VARIATIONS ON A HORSEY THEME

You can create all sorts of creatures using the basic stick-horse instructions. For example, add a horn to make a unicorn, teeth and a spikey crest to create a dragon, an orange mane to make a lion, stripes to make a zebra, or spots to create a jaguar.

Terry and José find the stick horses in the dramatic-play center and decide to ride horses. They each straddle a horse and begin to maneuver around the table. Terry has a baby doll under one arm that she wants to keep with her. She has some difficulty trying to hold the doll and the reins at the same time, and she drops the doll several times before finally finding a grip that works. "We're riding horses!" says José as they move around the room. "Giddyup!"

CREATING PROP BOXES FOR DRAMATIC PLAY

Children participate in dramatic activities by themselves, but when other children join in, magic happens! By definition, sociodramatic play occurs when two or more children work together to create a play frame. Whether pretending to be a family or engaging in a familiar social routine such as going to the grocery store, the opportunities for learning are endless. Sociodramatic plays allows children to work together to solve problems, negotiate social conflicts, plan, and imagine. They have opportunities to stretch their language abilities through role play and conversation as actors in their own dramas. Hidden learning opportunities include self-regulation, through having to control themselves to fit into the play scenario, and include the development of symbolic thinking, as their play becomes increasingly complex. This type of play also aids in their ability to see the perspectives of others. As a child pretends to be a doctor, she acts differently than she does when she is pretending to be the patient. When you add literacy props, children have the chance to pretend and explore the purposes of writing and calculating. Promote dramatic play and sociodramatic play by providing props related to themes that children enjoy.

Money Props

Researchers have found that when teachers incorporate literacy materials into children's play environments, children can practice and discover literate functions (Neuman and Roskos, 1997). For example, you might provide restaurant props that include menus, play money, order pads, and receipts. As children pretend to take orders and sign receipts, they will practice and enhance literacy skills that they will use throughout their lives.

The following is a list of ideas for creating a money prop box.

Play checks

Cash register

Purses and wallets

Money tray

Gift cards or credit cards

Receipts

MATERIALS IN ACTION—MONEY CONCEPTS

Armand appears to be organizing the play money in the tray. Tarana comes up and asks him for some. She is holding a purse and says that she needs it to go shopping. Armand says she can have five and proceeds to give her five bills of varying denominations. She asks how much it is, and he replies, "It's a hundred dollars! And that's a lot. But you can have more." He grabs a few more bills and then declares, "Now you have a million dollars. A million dollars!" She thanks him, puts it in the purse, and moves on to play.

Bakery Props

Create a bakery prop box using real objects, such as cookie cutters, cookie sheets, mixing bowls, wooden spoons, spatulas, cooling racks, cupcake tins and liners, rolling pins, cake pans, pie tins, birthday candles, wax paper, and bakery boxes. You can also add playdough, which the children can use in place of real dough.

To add literacy, math, and science elements, include cake size charts, pricing signs, money props, and a cash register. Make a menu book using labeled photos of cakes in a binder with page protectors. Add bakery order forms, recipe cards, and a keyboard and computer screen to the prop box, as well. Provide environmental print, such as a bakery sign and logo and empty cake-mix boxes, egg cartons, milk cartons, and frosting tubs.

Be sure to include aprons, chef hats, chef shirts, and oven mitts to complete the prop box.

MATERIALS IN ACTION—LETTER RECOGNITION

Jonas is playing with a disconnected keyboard by himself. He pushes the keys while saying the correct letter names in a random manner. Then he says, "I can do my name." For each letter in his name, he pushes the correct key while he says it out loud. Chandra comes over and is watching him. "Chandra, I can do your name. How do you spell your name?" Jonas asks. While Chandra says the letters in her name, Jonas pushes the correct keys. When he finishes, Chandra asks if she can try. Jonas pushes the keyboard toward her saying, "You can do my name now. It starts with J." Chandra sits down and begins typing Jonas's name as Jonas says the letters and helps her find the keys.

Thrifty Teacher's Guide to Creative Learning Centers

Veterinarian and Pet-Shop Props

Create a prop box for a veterinarian's office or pet shop by including real objects, such as a computer screen, keyboard, doctor kit, gauze, bandages, pet crates, feeding bowls, rawhide bones, a bird cage, a hamster habitat, stuffed toy animals, pet toys, grooming brushes or mitts, a tub or sensory table for pet baths, towels, and plastic cone collars.

Add literacy, math, and science elements with money props, a cash register, file folders with doctor's notes, a clipboard with a patient sign-in sheet, writing utensils, labeled pet-anatomy posters, and pet magazines for the waiting room. Include environmental print with local pet-shop or veterinary signs, advertisements or coupons for pet products, pet food and treat boxes, empty pet-shampoo bottles, and X-rays. Be sure to include doctors' coats and scrubs for the children to wear.

Ben and LaToya are seen playing with the foot-measuring device they found with the shoe-store props. They take turns putting their feet on it and talking about how they have big feet. Ben insists that his are really big. LaToya points out that their teacher's foot is really, really big. They ask her to come over and show them.

Shoe-Store Props

Create a shoe-store prop box using real objects such as gently used shoes, empty shoe boxes, tissue paper, a foot-measuring device, an unbreakable mirror positioned at foot level, open shelves, and chairs.

Add literacy, math, and science elements with money props, shoe-size charts, sale signs, a keyboard, and a computer screen. Include environmental print such as store signs and logos, advertisements, coupons, and junk mail. Provide dress-up clothes and accessories, as well.

Camping Props

Create a camping prop box with real objects such as children's tents, blankets, small sleeping bags, small ice chests, pots and pans, buckets, fishing lures, binoculars, and flashlights. Set the scene with real logs and stones and red, yellow, and orange tissue paper for a campfire. Add a poster board or fabric pond.

Include literacy, math, and science elements with magnetic fish, a poster and ruler for measuring fish, spiral notebooks for nature journals, and a book of bird images and names. Hang the same bird images around the room for viewing. Include environmental print using camping signs, maps, birdwatching guides, and star or constellation books.

You can create your own magnetic fish by printing or drawing images of fish and laminating the images. Add paper clips to the images, and secure the clips with tape. Write the name of each fish on the back of the image. Put the fish in the pond, and the children can go fishing using a magnet attached to the end of a length of string tied to a stick.

Include costumes such as fishing vests, hats, baseball caps, and hiking boots.

Several children are playing inside a tent that has been set up in the dramatic-play area of their classroom. The teachers overhear the children inside randomly yelling about a bear. Evidently it is big, has sharp teeth and gigantic claws, is going to get them, and they are scared. Saul pokes his head out of the door flap and looks directly at one of his teachers. With his fists clamped tightly in front of him and his eyes open wide, he whispers, "There's a bear! It's coming! Get inside!" Someone from inside the tent yells, "Shut the door! It's going to get you!" Saul yelps and ducks back inside.

Grocery-Store Props

Make a grocery-store prop box using real objects such as empty food boxes and containers, reusable shopping bags, plastic baskets, shopping carts, and paper sacks. Include literacy, math, and science elements with money props and a cash register. Add environmental print such as store signs and logos, advertisements, coupons, sale signs, and department signs such as *Produce*, *Meats*, *Dairy*, and so on.

Include uniforms or costumes, such as aprons, chef or butcher outfits, and so on.

Doctor and Hospital Props

Create a medical prop box using real objects such as doctor kits, bandages, exam paper for tables, dolls, a computer screen, a keyboard, and telephones. Add literacy, math, and science elements with a sign-in clipboard, file folders, writing materials for charts, and magazines and children's books for the waiting room. Include environmental print such as local hospital and clinic signs, prescription forms, an eye chart, a labeled skeleton poster, a form for doctor's notes, X-rays, and body diagrams. Provide costumes such as doctor coats, nurse uniforms, shoe covers, and surgical masks.

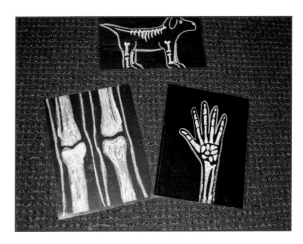

Flower-Shop Props

Make a flower-shop prop box using real objects such as artificial flowers, plastic vases, foam floral bricks, moss, plastic flower pots, tissue paper, gardening tools, watering pitchers, empty spray bottles, and plastic and wicker baskets. Add literacy, math, and science elements with order forms, floral cards and holders, money props, and a keyboard and computer screen. Include environmental print such as florist signs and logos. Provide aprons and gloves for the children to wear.

When it is time to clean up the pretend grocery-store area, Shelby takes it upon herself to line up the plastic bottles across the top of the shelf. The bottles are empty and tip over easily. As soon as she gets two side by side, a third one tips and knocks the others over like dominoes. She starts over and it happens again. She lets out a deep sigh and tries again. Eventually, she manages to get all five bottles lined up.

Restaurant Props

Make a restaurant prop box with real objects such as checkered tablecloths, plates, cups of various sizes, serving trays, plastic silverware, napkins, plastic pitchers, check presenters, and recycled take-out containers. Add literacy, math, and science elements with money props, order pads, menus, receipts, coupons, gift cards, and a wait-list clipboard. Include environmental print with local restaurant signs and logos. Add in aprons and a chef's costume.

On Monday morning, the preschoolers arrive to find restaurant props near the dramatic-play center. This area of the room quickly becomes very popular. The teachers enjoy observing the play from the sidelines. In addition to other props, the children can see signs from several restaurants in their community that have been taped onto the shelf holding the cash register. Mark and Pei Lee recognize the logos and point to them, calling each by name and saying which is their favorite. A well-known pancake house seems to be the winner. Pei Lee says she wants to go there and eat blueberry pancakes. Mark says he does not like blueberries. He likes strawberries.

4 Manipulatives

A parent donation of a bag of recycled bottle caps gives the preschool teachers the idea to simply place them in the classroom to see how the children might use them. Evie is the first to show real interest. She begins by sorting the caps into groups by color. A short while later, one of the teachers notices that Evie has placed the caps in twisty lines using one color at a time. Another child, Angela, comes over to watch and begins to help place the caps following the pattern Evie has started. Angela comments that there are more green caps than any other color and that there are almost as many red caps as green ones. Evie responds, "I know! I already counted them!"

Exploring and manipulating objects is one of the primary ways children learn about how the world works. It is natural for them to want to touch and hold objects they come across to explore how they feel and what they can do. What happens when you drop them, stack them, collect them, dump them? All of this helps build foundational concepts such as size, weight, number, and texture. When children have access to a pile of small objects, they are able to learn about more and less, a little or a lot. Open-ended opportunities lead to piling, sorting, classifying, quantifying, and lining up objects. From larger objects, such as blocks and dolls, to smaller ones, such as pebbles or counting bears, children need the experience of manipulating the objects themselves to build these concrete understandings (Hirsh-Pasek, Golinkoff, and Eyer, 2003). Other manipulatives, such as matching cards and folder games, provide children with opportunities to problem solve and work from memory. Provide puzzles and other manipulatives that match children's abilities so they can practice the skills they are mastering. Increasingly challenge children as their competency level grows. Often, either the teacher or another child will provide scaffolding assistance. Children develop the leading edge of their competency in interaction with others—what they can do today with help from a teacher or a friend they can do by themselves tomorrow. From puzzles with real pictures or storybook themes to parquetry blocks or peg boards, manipulatives provide children with skills they will use throughout their lives.

INVITING CHILDREN TO EXPLORE MANIPULATIVES

Enhance children's learning by providing a wide variety of materials and rotating them frequently based on the children's interest and engagement. Displaying manipulative materials in interesting baskets and trays will pique children's interest to explore. For example, display an assortment of shells in wicker baskets or provide pompoms in a muffin tin with tongs that children can discover when they arrive.

Observe children as they engage with manipulative materials to determine the appropriate difficulty level. If the children finish an activity or puzzle quickly and easily, it may be time to provide a greater challenge. You can also connect the theme of a manipulative material to curriculum interests. A classroom interest in vegetables and gardening might lead to making a vegetable puzzle or garden-tool matching cards.

MANIPULATIVE PLAY SUPPORTS LEARNING ACROSS DOMAINS

As children engage with manipulative materials, they have many opportunities to build on their emerging skills in language and literacy development; physical development; social and emotional development; and science, math, and cognitive development.

Children have opportunities to build on their language skills as they talk to themselves and converse with others, as they name the materials they are working with, and as they use new vocabulary related to materials or themes in the materials such as a photograph on a puzzle. Play with manipulative materials enhances eye-hand coordination through manipulating materials or the pieces to a puzzle. When children put pieces together or arrange them in novel ways, they build fine motor skills. Children have opportunities to build on their social skills when cooperating and negotiating with others as they use and share materials.

Emotional development is enhanced when children work through strong emotions such as frustration while trying to figure out a problem, or when they experience the satisfaction that comes with completing a game or puzzle. They develop persistence as they work to finish activities.

As they engage with manipulatives, children have opportunities to further their cognitive skills when matching letters, numerals, or objects for a game. They build on their science understandings as they develop concepts about size, shape, and other attributes of objects. Math learning is enhanced through opportunities to count objects. The following lists manipulative materials typically found in preschool classrooms.

- Materials for sorting and counting, such as counting bears or pompoms
- Sorting bins or trays
- Puzzles
- Matching or memory cards
- Lacing or weaving materials
- Board games
- Peg boards

COLLECT MATERIALS AND CONTAINERS TO SUPPORT USE OF MANIPULATIVES

Collect sets of related materials and containers that can be used for manipulative play. Not only can interesting containers and trays create an attractive invitation, they also will be used by children to sort, divide, and categorize the materials. Many recycled objects, such as egg cartons or party trays with dividing slots, naturally lend themselves to manipulative play. The following lists ideas for loose parts and sorting containers to add to your classroom:

- Sand timers
- Nuts and bolts
- Locks and keys
- Buttons
- Seashells
- Pebbles
- Beads
- Paper clips
- Golf tees
- Plastic bottle caps
- Chenille stems
- Poker chips
- Acorns
- Seeds
- Small toy animals
- Novelty erasers

MATERIALS IN ACTION—SORTING

Evan notices a pile of colorful bottle caps that his teacher has been collecting on top of the manipulatives shelf. He spends some time manipulating and sliding them around. Then he begins sorting them into two piles by size. Next, he re-sorts them by color. After he has sorted for a while, he begins lining them up in a row that stretches across the top of the shelf. When he comes to the end, he curves the line and heads back in the other direction. He is careful in his placement, and it appears that he is trying to keep the space between the caps even.

- Ice-cube tray
- Egg carton
- Muffin tins
- Recycled plastic fruit tray
- Wicker basket with sections
- Plastic jewelry boxes
- Plastic containers with sections
- Party platters
- Sectioned plates
- Lunch trays
- Egg plates
- Empty bulk crayon box
- Paper cups
- Plastic bowls or cups

MATERIALS IN ACTION—NUMERAL RECOGNITION

David and Rikki are using pebbles to fill in a laminated number chart. The numerals 1 to 8 are in a vertical column on the left side of the chart, and there are spaces next to each numeral that indicate the correct number of items to match the numeral. David places one pebble in each space. Rikki seems to be keeping track as David works. She says, "You finished seven. The next one is eight. You have to put eight on it. It's the last one and then you did it!"

Thrifty Teacher's Guide to Creative Learning Centers

In addition to providing loose parts for manipulative play, you can create materials that require children to flex their hand muscles and strengthen their fine motor skills through opening and closing, stacking, bending, and fitting pieces together. The children will enjoy exploring the textures and learning to manipulate the materials.

Manipulative Board

Materials

Plywood scrap, 10" x 12"	Small screws
	2 small hinges
Plywood scrap, 4" x 4"	Screwdriver
Paint	Hot-glue gun
Paintbrush	(adult use only)
Slide latch	Drill and large drill bit
Hook-and-eye latch	(adult use only)
Light switch	Sandpaper
Zipper	Acrylic paint

1. Sand the rough edges from the plywood scraps. Paint the boards as desired.

2. Screw on a variety of hinges and latches.

3. Using the drill, cut a small hole into the board for the light switch to fit into. Attach the switch with screws.

4. Attach a zipper using a hot-glue gun.

Felt Rings

Materials

Felt in a variety of colors
Adhesive Velcro tape
Hot-glue gun (adult use only)

1. Cut the felt into 1-inch strips.

2. Cut the Velcro tape into 1-inch squares.

3. Use hot glue to attach the Velcro squares onto the ends of the felt strips.

4. The children can connect the rings into chains or explore other ways to use them.

Hat Bands

Materials

Recycled food canisters   Scissors

Colored duct tape   Ponytail holders

Craft foam

1. Cover the food canisters with duct tape.

2. Cut circles from the craft foam in larger diameters than the food canisters.

3. Place a canister on a foam circle to imitate a stovepipe-style hat.

4. Children can slide the ponytail holders over the canister to create different hats.

Marble Maze

Materials

Marbles   caps, corks, and

Large box lid, such as a   plastic lids

    copy paper lid   Craft sticks

Assorted recycled items,   Straws

    such as food-pouch   Hot-glue gun

                           (adult use only)

1. Use hot glue to attach the recycled items, craft sticks, and straws to create a maze for the marbles. Let the children direct where the items should be attached.

2. Show the children how to place a marble in the maze and move the box lid to roll the marble.

Pool Noodle Connectors

Materials

Perforated   Pool noodles

   plastic balls   Scissors

1. Cut the pool noodles into half-inch strips of varying sizes.

2. Use scissors to taper the ends of the strips so they fit into the holes in the perforated plastic balls.

3. Encourage the children to build structures by connecting the balls with the pool-noodle strips.

Todd and Raquel are interested in the materials they find set up on a table. There is a polystyrene block, golf tees, and marbles. They push the golf tees into the foam in a random manner, chatting as they work. Raquel starts placing marbles on top of the tees. It's a little tricky, as she keeps accidently knocking off marbles as she tries to place new ones. Added to that is the way the whole piece of foam moves as Todd continues to poke in more golf tees. Raquel asks him to stop shaking it. He tells her that he will try. They both continue their tasks a little longer before Todd leaves the table. Raquel continues a little longer before moving on herself.

CREATE MATERIALS FOR MATCHING

Matching materials provide children with opportunities to visually discriminate different sizes, colors, shapes, and patterns. As you observe the children, you will be able to determine the degree of difficulty that will enhance children's learning.

Bingo

Materials

Card stock Scissors

Glue Counting bears or other

Magazines or store flyers small items

1. Create bingo cards using a word-processing program to make 3 x 3 tables of large squares.

2. Print the grids on card stock for added durability.

3. Cut out images from magazines or store flyers. These can be selected based on themes you wish to emphasize, such as animals, things you find in a kitchen, foods, garden tools, and so on.

4. Glue an image in each space on the bingo cards. Be sure to leave the center square empty, and write *FREE* in it.

5. Create a set of images that will be the calling cards. Glue images that match (or closely resemble) the images used on the bingo cards onto the calling cards.

Silhouette Matching

Materials

Patterned paper   Scissors

Construction paper   Glue

Recycled lacing buttons
    or other repurposed
    items

1. Create silhouette matching cards by tracing the outlines of lacing buttons onto construction paper.
2. Cut out the shapes, and glue them onto pieces of patterned paper.

3. Encourage the children to match the lacing buttons with the paper shapes.

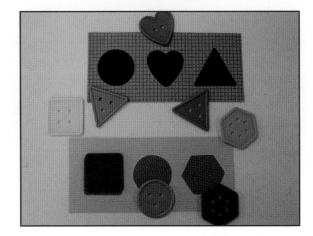

Paint-Chip Matching

Materials

Paint-chip cards   Scissors

Clothespins   Glue

1. Using a paint-chip card with multiple shades of one color, cut a narrow strip from one edge of the paint-chip card.
2. Cut the strip into individual shades.
3. Glue each shade onto a clothespin.
4. Encourage the children to clip the clothespins onto the paint-chip cards on the matching colors.

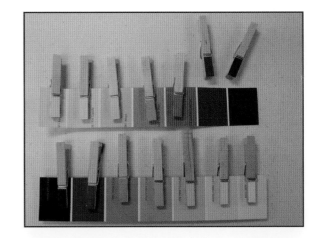

Matching Sticks

Materials

Jumbo craft sticks

Permanent markers

1. Place two craft sticks together, and use markers to make patterns that extend to both sticks. Repeat with more sticks.
2. Encourage the children to match the craft sticks by pattern.

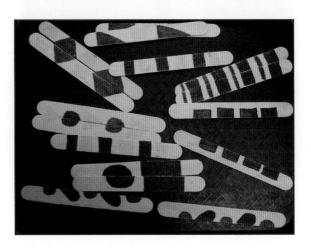

Rose, Alexei, and Audrey are playing their own version of bingo with the farm-animal bingo game their teacher made. Alexei has placed the calling cards facedown on the table, and as he picks them up one at a time, he says the animal's name. Rose and Audrey either cheer or groan, depending on whether they are able to make a match. After a few more calls, Audrey jumps up, yelling, "Bingo! Bingo! Bingo!" Both girls empty their cards. Audrey lets Alexei know that it is her turn to call since she was the winner. Alexei picks up a bingo card so they can begin another game.

Color-Matching Eggs

Materials

Plastic eggs

White felt

Felt scraps that match the colors of the plastic eggs

1. Cut white felt into shapes that resemble egg whites.

2. Cut circles of colored felt to resemble egg yolks.

3. Glue the yolks onto the egg whites.

4. Encourage the children to match the eggs with the egg whites and yolks.

MATCHING AND MEMORY CARDS

For younger preschoolers, these cards are just fun to match. As they progress, children can turn the cards over to play a memory game. The cards are simple to make when you have two matching sets of images. Some ideas include the following:

- Stickers
- Real-estate guides
- Store flyers
- Magazines

Tip: You can use a color copier to duplicate if you only have one set of images.

CREATE PUZZLES

Puzzles naturally provide opportunities for problem solving, trial and error, and concept development. Children have to think about what the puzzle will look like when finished as they are putting it together, which aids in their ability to think abstractly. There are many different ways teachers can make puzzles that match the children's skills and then help them reach the next level. For example, cut a photograph into pieces for the children to reassemble. Glue a photo onto a paper plate, and cut the plate into sections. Draw a simple image, such as a boat, onto a paint-chip card. Write the word for the image beneath the image, and cut the card into strips.

Craft-Stick Puzzles

Materials
10 craft sticks
Permanent markers
Magazine
Scissors
Glue

1. Lay the craft sticks side-by-side in a row.

2. Draw your own picture with the markers, or cut a photo into ten strips and place the pieces on the craft sticks.

3. If using a magazine photo, decoupage one photo piece onto each craft stick.

4. Using a marker, number each craft stick.

5. Encourage the children to put the puzzle images together.

Interlocking Block Puzzles

Materials

Large plastic interlocking blocks

Magazine

Scissors

Tape

1. Create a simple puzzle to add to the fun in the block or manipulatives area. Gather several photos from a magazine or the Internet.

2. Cut the photos in halves.

3. Tape each half onto an interlocking block to create a stackable puzzle.

Green Eggs Shape Puzzle

Materials

Green craft foam

Scissors

Poster board

Green marker

Ruler

1. On a piece of poster board, draw several outlines to resemble an egg cracked onto a surface.

2. Cut shapes from the craft foam: square, circle, triangle, rhombus, and so on.

3. Within each egg outline, trace one of the shapes.

4. Encourage the children to match the foam shapes to the outlines on the poster board.

Tiffany is at the table manipulating the laminated pie puzzles that are spread out in front of her. Some of the pies are whole, some cut in half, and some cut in fourths. "I'm making mixed-up pies," she says to no one in particular. "This one is half pumpkin and half blueberry," she says as she lines up the pieces. Next, she puts together a half piece with two quarter pieces. "This one is half pumpkin and half blueberry and half apple!"

Wooden Block Puzzle

Materials

6 wooden blocks	Glue
Magazine	Water
Scissors	Bowl
Pencil	Paintbrush

1. Print or cut out an image you would like to use.

2. Turn the photo over, and place the blocks on the photo in a 3 x 3 group.

3. Trace around the whole puzzle area.

4. Trim the edges of the photo, following the traced lines.

5. Trace around the individual blocks, and cut the individual pieces.

6. Create the decoupage solution by mixing one part white glue to one part water.

7. Using an old paintbrush, cover one surface of a block.

8. Place the image piece in the desired spot, and brush the decoupage mixture over the image.

9. Continue until all six of the blocks contain a part of the puzzle image.

10. Allow to dry overnight.

Variations: Cut a vertical image into three parts, and glue them to a stack of three blocks. Make several and encourage the children to mix and match the pieces.

Instead of wooden cube blocks, use oblong wooden blocks.

CREATE FOLDER GAMES

Folder games can become a favorite activity of preschoolers when they build on the children's interests. You can create folders that relate to those interests, curriculum topics, or general skills the children are working to master. Use the games to promote a variety of skills from visual and shape discrimination to letter recognition and more.

Leaf Silhouettes

Materials

File folder	Scissors
Set of images, such as leaves	Glue
Black paper	Pencil
Adhesive Velcro tape	Clear contact paper

1. Cut out the desired images.

2. Place an image onto black paper, and trace around it.

3. Cut out the silhouetted image.

4. Glue the silhouetted image to the file folder in a random pattern. Repeat with the other silhouettes.

5. Laminate or cover the images and folder with clear contact paper for durability. Trim any excess.

6. Cut squares of adhesive Velcro. Place half of a Velcro piece onto a silhouette. Place the other half onto the back of the matching image. **Tip:** Be consistent in putting the hooked halves on the images and the looped halves on the black silhouettes.

Apple Bushel Counting

Materials

Photos of apples	Scissors
Photos of bushel baskets	Glue
File folder	Permanent marker

1. Cut out the bushel baskets, and glue them to the inside of the folder.

2. Cut out the apples.

3. Laminate both the folder and the apples.

4. Use a permanent marker to number the bushel baskets. You can use numbers that you know the children are learning. Next to each number, draw that number of dots.

5. Encourage the children to place the correct number of apples in the bushel baskets.

Cupcake Letter Match

Materials

File folder

Construction paper in two colors

Glue

Scissors

Permanent marker

1. Create a template for the cupcake holders and cut out twenty-six.

2. Create a template for the tops of the cupcakes and cut out twenty-six.

3. Label the cupcake holders with uppercase letters and the cupcake tops with lowercase letters.

4. Glue the holders to the file folder.

5. Laminate the folder and the cupcake toppers.

6. Encourage the children to match the lowercase letters with the uppercase letters.

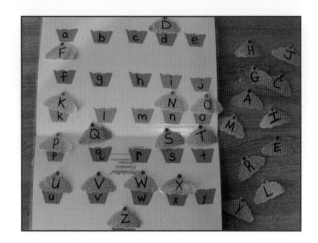

Pet Matching

Materials

File folder

2 each of eight images, such as dogs

Scissors

Glue

Clear contact paper

Dry-erase or water-soluble markers

1. Glue one set of images in a column on the left side of the open file folder.

2. Glue the other set in a column on the right side in an order different from your column on the left.

3. Laminate the folder or cover it in clear contact paper.

4. Children can use the markers to connect the matching images.

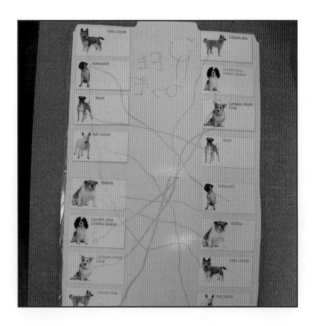

Pumpkin Counting

Materials

Small objects to count, such as plastic pumpkins
Photo of a similar object
File folder
Glue
Scissors
Permanent marker
Clear contact paper

1. Print or duplicate the image ten times.

2. Cut out the images, and glue them to the file folder.

3. Use permanent marker to number the images, then laminate or cover the folder with clear contact paper.

4. Encourage the children to place the appropriate number of objects on the images.

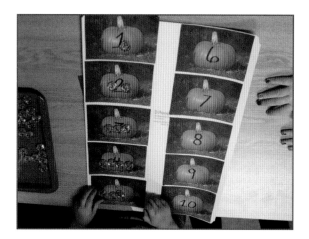

Pattern Discrimination Kites

Materials

File folder
Assorted patterned paper
Yarn
Adhesive Velcro tape
Hot-glue gun (adult use only)
Glue
Scissors
Clear contact paper

1. Cut two kite shapes from each of several different pieces of patterned paper.

2. Glue one of each pair on to the file folder.

3. Laminate the folder and the other set of kite shapes, or cover them with clear contact paper.

4. Use hot glue to attach yarn tails to each kite.

5. Cut squares of Velcro tape. Attach the hook side of the squares to the kites on the folder and the loop sides to the kite pieces.

What Will You Pack in Your Suitcase?

Materials

File folder

Glue

Scissors

Magazines

Clear contact paper

1. Find images in magazines that include items you would typically pack in a suitcase, such as clothing. Find other images that you would not pack, such as elephants or vacuum cleaners. Cut out a variety of images.

2. Cut a small oval-shaped hole in the top of the file folder so that the file folder resembles an open suitcase.

3. Laminate the file folder and images, or cover them with clear contact paper.

4. Encourage the children to pack a suitcase and to talk about what they choose.

Five Little Chickadees

Materials

File folder

Bird image

Glue

Scissors

Adhesive Velcro tape

Clear contact paper

1. Write the lyrics to the song on the file folder, or print a typed version and glue it to the file folder.

2. Write the numerals 1 to 5 on the inside of the folder.

3. Cut out five identical bird images.

4. Laminate the file folder and birds, or cover them with clear contact paper.

5. Cut squares of Velcro tape. Attach the hook side of the tape to the birds. Attach the loop side to the folder above the numerals.

6. Children can sing the song while removing and replacing birds.

Variation: Create additional folders using similar songs such as "Five Little Pumpkins" or "Five Little Ducks."

Ellie is playing with a folder game of the "Five Little Chickadees" song. The birds are laminated pieces that attach to the folder with Velcro tape. As she sings the song, she removes a bird each time it is supposed to fly away. At first there are five birds sitting by the door. One flies away and then there are four. She continues through each part of the rhyming song until all of the birds have flown away.

Name Matching Game

Materials

Set of small photos of the children in your classroom

File folder

Scissors

Glue

Adhesive Velcro tape

White card stock

Clear contact paper

1. Cut small rectangles from the white card stock, and label each with a child's name.

2. Cut out the children's photos, and glue them onto the file folder.

3. Laminate the folder and name pieces, or cover them with clear contact paper.

4. Cut squares of Velcro tape. Attach the hook side to the folder near each child's photo, and attach the loop side to the backs of children's name pieces.

5. Encourage the children to match the names and faces of their classmates.

CREATE MATERIALS FOR LACING AND STRINGING

Lacing beads, cards, and buttons are traditional materials in preschool classrooms, as they assist children in developing fine motor skills and eye-hand coordination. Children also begin to recognize and create their own patterns. Build on this idea by creating lacing and stringing activities that relate to the children's interests or curriculum themes. The following are lists of items that you could include.

Materials for Lacing

▦ Shoestrings

▦ Yarn

▦ Twine

▦ Chenille stems

▦ Craft feathers

- Straws
- Ribbons
- Coffee stir sticks

Objects for Stringing

- *O*-shaped cereal
- Pony beads

- Wooden craft beads
- Recycled thread spools
- Large buttons

Tip: Whenever you use food in the classroom, make sure that the children have an opportunity to eat it after the activity!

Shoe-Tying Boards

Materials

Scrap pieces of thin plywood
Acrylic paint or permanent markers
Drill (adult use only)
Shoelaces
Sandpaper

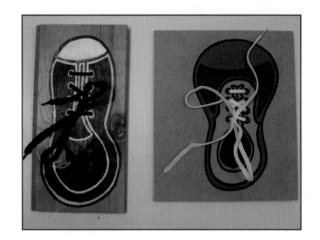

1. Sand the rough edges of the plywood.

2. Draw a shoe shape on the wood, and color it with permanent marker or paint.

3. Use a drill to make holes where the shoes will be laced.

Tissue-Box Lacing

Materials

Recycled tissue box   Hole punch
Duct tape   Shoelace

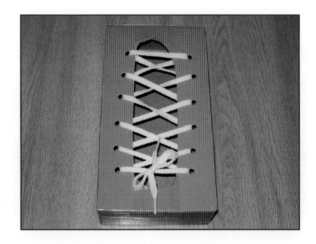

1. Cover the tissue box with duct tape to reinforce it. Be sure to leave the box opening uncovered.

2. Use a hole punch along each edge of the opening to create the lacing holes.

3. Provide a long shoelace that the children can use for lacing up the box.

Foam-Curler Stringing

Materials

Foam curlers   Scissors   Shoelaces

1. Remove the foam from the curlers. Recycle the plastic clips.

2. Cut the foam into 1-inch pieces.

3. Provide shoelaces and encourage the children to string the foam pieces on the shoelace.

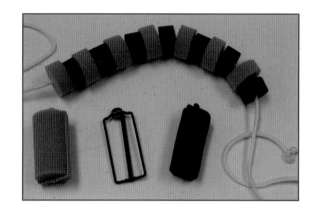

Mini Tree-Cookie Stringing

Materials

Tree branches with 1-inch diameter
Hand saw (adult use only)
Drill (adult use only)
Shoelaces

1. Use the handsaw to cut tree cookies with a thickness of less than a half inch.

2. Drill a hole in the center of each tree cookie.

3. Provide shoelaces, and encourage the children to string the tree cookies.

Lacing Cards

Materials

Craft foam or vinyl placemats   Shoelaces
Hole punch

1. Cut the craft foam or placemats into various shapes. For example, you can cut out squares, triangles, circles, and so on. Or, you can cut out letters that the children are learning.

2. Hole punch around the edge of each shape.

3. Provide shoelaces, and encourage the children to lace through the holes. If they wish, the children can string the shapes together.

Variation: Cards can also be made from laminated card stock. Use the hole punch after laminating.

Several children are sitting together at a table stringing beads. Two of the children appear to be adding beads to their shoestrings in a random manner, but Marisol chooses a pattern card that her teacher has made. The pattern cards show photos of beads in specific patterns, such as AB, ABC, AAB, and so on. She spends time searching for the correct color and shape of beads to complete the sequence exactly as it is on the card. When finished, she chooses another card to work on.

Chenille Stems and Beads

Materials

Chenille stems

Beads in a variety of colors

Alphabet beads

1. Provide chenille stems and beads for the children to string.

2. Encourage the children to create a variety of patterns. Talk with them as they work, and ask them to describe their patterns.

3. Encourage the children to use the alphabet beads to create words, such as *Mom* or the children's names.

COLLECT AND CREATE MATERIALS FOR WEAVING

Weaving provides children with the opportunity to use more than one lace or string. When children have opportunities to weave materials, they begin to recognize complex patterns while enhancing their fine motor skills and eye-hand coordination. The following lists ideas for weaving materials.

◼ Shoe strings

◼ Yarn

- Twine
- Chenille stems
- Ribbon
- Thin lace
- Rickrack

- Plastic baskets
- Colander
- Paper plate protectors
- Sink Mat
- Cooling rack

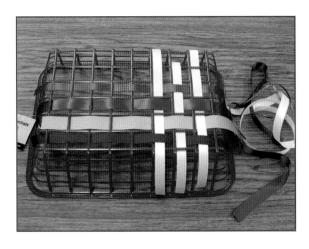

COLLECT AND CREATE MATERIALS TO SUPPORT LITERACY LEARNING

When teachers collect and create manipulatives that display the alphabet, they provide opportunities for children to explore and recognize letters in an open-ended manner. Children will begin to match letters, find the initial letters of their names, and then move on to finding all the letters in their names. Many teachers prioritize activities that utilize children's names because they recognize that children have a natural interest in their names. This is a great segue to interest in the alphabet in general. Once children know and recognize the letters in their own name, they have a head start on the rest of the alphabet.

Letter Scramble

Materials
Recycled game tiles, such as Scrabble tiles

1. Encourage the children to find the first letters of their names.

2. Let them explore combining the letters in different ways. Talk with them about the letter sounds.

Sand Letter Search

Materials

Plastic tray   Recycled game tiles,
Play sand   such as Scrabble tiles

1. Pour sand into the tray, covering the entire surface.

2. Hide letters in the sand.

3. Encourage the children to find the letters and to name the ones they find. Talk about the sound each letter makes.

Letter Sticks

Materials

26 craft sticks   Construction paper
Tape or glue   Scissors

1. Cut out letters from the construction paper.

2. Cut a small piece of construction paper, and glue a letter onto it.

3. Tape the letter onto the end of a craft stick.

4. Repeat, creating letter sticks for each letter of the alphabet.

5. Encourage the children to combine the letters in different ways. As they work, talk with

them about the letter names and the letter sounds.

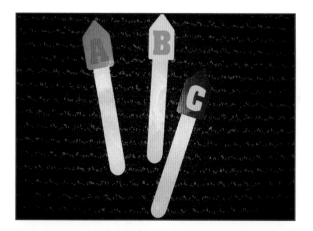

Alphabet Clothespin Match

Materials

Alphabet chart   Permanent marker
26 wooden clothespins

1. On each clothespin, write a letter of the alphabet. Depending on what you are teaching, write both the uppercase and lowercase letters, or just write one or the other.

2. Encourage the children to clip a clothespin onto the bottom of the chart just below the

matching letter. Talk about the letter names and the sounds they make.

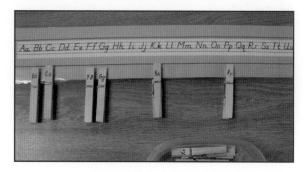

Letter-Eating Monster

Materials

Recycled shoe box

Construction paper

Scissors

Tape or glue

Clear contact paper

1. Cut a hole in the lid of the shoebox to create a mouth.

2. Decorate the box to resemble a monster.

3. Cut twenty-six circles from the construction paper, and write a letter on each.

4. Laminate or cover the letters with clear contact paper for added durability.

5. Encourage the children to feed alphabet letters to the monster, talking about the letters as they play.

Alphabet Match

Materials

Construction paper or butcher paper

Index cards or printer

Marker

Foam letters

Clear contact paper

1. Cut four pieces of construction paper in half lengthwise, and tape them together end to end to create a long strip. Or simply cut a strip of butcher paper.

2. Create an alphabet chart by drawing or printing the letters of the alphabet.

3. Cut out each letter and glue it onto the paper strip.

4. Cover the alphabet chart in clear contact paper or laminate it for durability.

5. Encourage the children to match the foam letters to the letters on the chart.

Name Drop

Materials

Recycled canister, such as for coffee creamer or
   sugar

Duct tape or Washi tape

Craft sticks

Permanent markers

1. Cover the canister with duct or Washi tape or
   other decoration.

2. Color the craft sticks.

3. With a black marker, write each child's name
   on a craft stick.

4. Place the name sticks in a basket, and
   encourage the children to find their own

name and the names of their classmates to
drop in the canister.

Name Match

Materials

Small photographs of the children in your
   classroom

Colored card stock

White card stock

Adhesive Velcro tape

Clear contact paper

1. Cut the white card stock into 1-inch squares.

2. For each child's name, label squares with the
   letters from that name—one letter per square.
   You will need two letter sets for each child.
   These could also be typed and printed.

3. From the colored card stock, cut a rectangle
   card long enough to fit a child's photo with
   her name.

4. Glue the photo on the left side of the
   rectangle and the child's name across the top.

5. Laminate or cover the name cards and the
   individual letters with clear contact paper.

6. Repeat until you have created a card and
   collection of letters for each child.

7. Cut squares from the Velcro tape.

8. Attach the hook side of the Velcro to the
   individual letters and the loop side to the card
   underneath the letters on the name card.

Thrifty Teacher's Guide to Creative Learning Centers

An assistant teacher made name puzzles for each child. At the morning meeting the next day, she let the children know she had made name puzzles for everyone in the classroom and that they could find their puzzles on the manipulatives shelf during free-choice time. When the time came, several children went searching for their puzzles. Laurie and José quickly found theirs and put them together before moving on to another activity in the room. Christopher dumped the pieces of his puzzle on the table and immediately asked the teacher for help, but she was busy and said she would come over when she could. While he waited, he began putting his puzzle together using his name written on the front of the envelope as a guide. By the time the teacher got there, he had completed the puzzle and proudly showed it to her.

Name Puzzles

Materials

Sentence strips   Scissors

Permanent marker   Clear contact paper

Envelopes

1. Create a name puzzle for each child in your classroom by writing each name on a sentence strip. Leave some space between each letter.

2. Laminate or cover the strips with clear contact paper for durability.

3. Create puzzle pieces by cutting between each letter in a zigzag or wavy pattern.

4. Store each child's puzzle in an envelope labeled with his name.

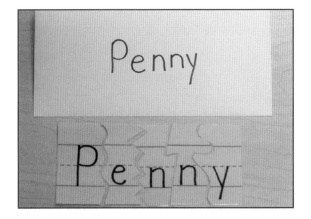

Name Clips

Materials

Jumbo craft sticks   Permanent marker

Clothespins

1. Write the letters of each child's name on a craft stick, leaving some space between each letter.

2. Write the letters of their names on individual clothespins.

3. Encourage the children to clip the matching letter onto each letter of their names.

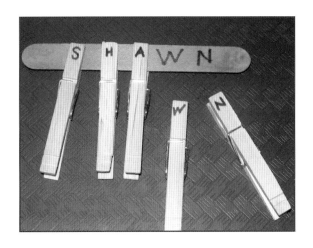

Chapter 4: Manipulatives

COLLECT AND CREATE MANIPULATIVES FOR COUNTING AND EXPLORING NUMERALS

You can collect materials, such as dominoes and playing cards, that lend themselves to counting and exploring numerals. You can also create materials with numerals. For example, use a permanent marker to write numerals on flat objects such as rocks, or create other numeral activities that will engage the children in exploring number concepts. The following lists ideas for materials you can use to encourage number explorations.

- Playing cards
- Calculator or adding machine
- Play money
- Computer keyboard
- Rolls of admission tickets
- Coupons
- Dominoes
- Dice
- Abacus

Clothespin Numeral Match

Materials
Construction paper   Marker
Clothespins   Ruler

1. On a sheet of construction paper, use a ruler to measure the desired number of spaces.

2. Create a number line by writing a numeral in each space.

3. On the clothespins, write one numeral each to match what you wrote on the number line.

4. Encourage the children to clip a clothespin onto the paper in the spot with the matching numeral.

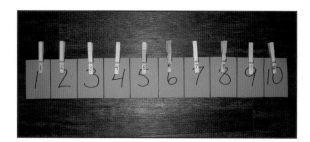

Candy Numeral Match

Materials
Recycled heart-shaped   Tube of glitter or
  candy box   puffy paint
Brown craft foam   Permanent marker

1. Use a permanent marker to label each space in a heart-shaped candy box with a different numeral.

2. Cut a piece of brown foam in the shape of each space.

3. Label each foam piece with the corresponding number using glitter or puffy paint.

4. Encourage the children to match the craft-foam candy pieces to the corresponding empty spaces.

French-Fry Count

Materials

Yellow sponges
French-fry containers
Small dot stickers
Permanent marker
Scissors

1. Cut the sponges into strips to resemble french fries.

2. On the front of each container, add a number of dots to represent a numeral.

3. On each container, write the corresponding numeral next to the dots.

4. Encourage the children to count the corresponding number of french-fry sponges to match the numeral on the container.

Tip: You can find french-fry containers at dollar stores, or your local fast-food restaurant may donate some to your classroom.

Counting Wheels

Materials

White poster board or construction paper
Tiny stickers
Permanent marker
Ruler
10 clothespins
Clear contact paper

1. Cut circles with an 8-inch diameter from white poster board or construction paper.

2. Use a ruler and marker to draw dividing lines to make ten equal pie-shaped spaces.

3. Add stickers to each section to represent the numerals 1 to 10.

4. Laminate the wheel or cover it in clear contact paper.

5. Write the numerals from 1 to 10 on clothespins.

6. Encourage the children to clip a numeral clothespin onto the section with the corresponding number of stickers.

7. Create a variety of counting wheels using different stickers that can be used with the single set of clothespins.

Counting Graph

Materials

Ruler

Paper

Markers

Small items for counting, such as pebbles or counting bears

1. Create a numbered bar graph. On the Y axis, write the numerals 1 to 8 (or whichever numbers you are teaching).

2. For each numeral, draw and color in the corresponding number of squares on the graph. Of course, you can just create a graph on your computer and print it.

3. Cover the graph with clear contact paper or laminate it for durability.

4. Encourage the children to place a counter in each square as they count across the graph.

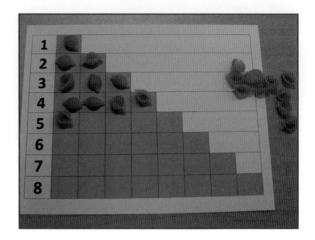

Bowling Pin Number Match

Materials

6 recycled plastic bottles

Sand

Colored masking tape

Poster board

Permanent marker

Playground ball

Clear contact paper

1. Wrap the bottles with masking tape.

2. Label each bottle with a numeral from 1 to 6.

3. Add one cup sand to each bottle to add weight.

4. Draw circles on poster board in a bowling-pin pattern.

5. Laminate the poster board or cover it with clear contact paper.

6. Children can match the numerals on the bottles to the numerals on the poster board to set up the pins. Then, they can bowl with the playground ball.

Dog Bones

Materials

Recycled tissue box	White paper
Duct tape, Washi tape, or recycled wrapping paper	Scissors
	Glue
	Clear contact paper
Dog image	

1. Create a small dog bone template on white paper, and cut out twenty bones.

2. Laminate the dog bones or cover them with clear contact paper.

3. Cut a hole in the bottom of the tissue box.

4. Cover the tissue box with duct tape, washi tape, or wrapping paper, leaving the openings on the top and bottom uncovered.

5. Glue the dog image to the top of the box over the opening. Cut a slit in the dog's mouth large enough to slide the bones through.

6. Encourage the children to count bones as they "feed" the dog. Bones can easily be retrieved from the hole in the bottom of the tissue box.

Variations: You could have a horse eating apples, a seal eating fish, or a chimpanzee eating bananas.

Number Matching

Materials

Construction paper

Dot stickers

Marker

Stickers

Clear contact paper

1. Cut ten 8-inch pieces from construction paper.

2. On each piece, write a numeral from 1 to 10 on the left side. Place the corresponding number of dot stickers on the right side.

3. Laminate or cover the pieces with clear contact paper.

4. Cut each piece in half using wavy or zigzag patterns to resemble puzzle pieces.

5. Children can either match the pieces as puzzles or count the dot stickers and match the piece with the corresponding numeral.

Allison is sitting on the floor playing with the dog-and-bones manipulative that one of her teachers has made. Allison is feeding the dog the laminated paper dog bones. When she runs out, she opens the box and dumps them out to begin again. She does this several times. Her teacher overhears her counting the bones as she feeds them into the dog's mouth. She gets all the way to twenty before running out of bones.

Cardboard Abacus

Materials

Cardboard scrap

Nylon string

Pony beads

Duct tape

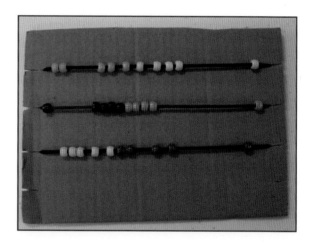

1. Cut a rectangle from cardboard. Cut slits on each side at equal distances.

2. Cut nylon string into pieces that are three times the length of the cardboard rectangle.

3. Slide ten pony beads onto each string.

4. Wrap each string around the cardboard so that the beads are in front and the string is in a slit on each side. Tie a knot in back.

5. Cover the knots with duct tape for added durability.

CREATE MATERIALS TO EXPLORE PATTERN AND SEQUENCE

When children engage with sets of loose parts, they naturally begin to make patterns and put items in varying sequences. Create materials that promote these particular skills.

Food-Pouch-Cap Pattern Cards

Materials

Hole punch with a	Glue
1 1/4-inch circle, or	Card stock
large circle stickers	Food-pouch caps
Colored paper	Clear contact paper

1. If you are using a hole punch, punch circles from the colored paper.

2. Glue the circles to the card stock, or place the stickers in designs or patterns on the cards.

3. Laminate or cover the cards with clear contact paper for added durability.

4. Encourage the children to re-create the patterns using the food-pouch lids.

Variation: You could also create circle pattern cards on your computer.

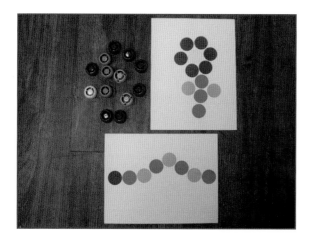

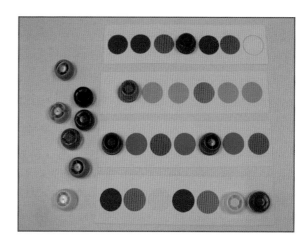

Pattern Cards

Materials

Lacing beads	Card stock
String	Glue
Digital camera	Scissors
Paper	Clear contact paper

1. String the beads in a pattern.

2. Take a picture of the pattern, and print it.

3. Cut out the photograph, and glue it onto card stock.

4. Create as many pattern cards as you wish.

5. Laminate or cover the cards with clear contact paper for added durability.

6. Encourage the children to re-create the bead patterns.

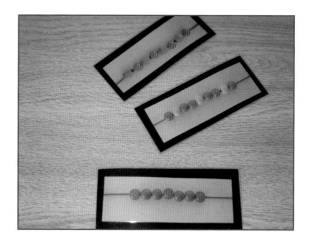

Interlocking-Block Pattern Cards

Materials

Colored paper   Glue

White card stock   Clear contact paper

Scissors

1. From colored paper, cut out block shapes the same size as your interlocking blocks.

2. Glue the block shapes onto card stock to create a building template. Create as many templates as you wish.

3. Laminate or cover each template with clear contact paper for added durability.

4. Add the templates to the block center, and encourage the children to re-create the block patterns.

Variation: You can also create your own pattern cards on the computer.

Magnetic Paper-Clip Patterns

Materials

Adhesive magnetic tape

Jumbo paper clips in a variety of colors

Jumbo craft sticks

1. Cut strips of magnetic tape, and attach them to the craft sticks.

2. Encourage the children to create patterns using the paper clips.

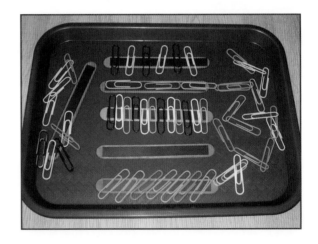

5 Art Materials

The children arrive to find an assortment of materials set out on a table, including purple paint; paintbrushes; paper; colored glue; and a variety of small sticks, shells, leaves, and rocks. Stephan and Aleena immediately sit down and get busy. Stephan begins using the purple paint on paper while Aleena uses it to paint a leaf. As they work, they talk about what each of them is doing. Stephan points out that Aleena has already painted "like fifty leafs." Aleena compliments Stephan's painting. He tells her he is making a mountain where superheroes live and then begins a long, detailed story about the superheroes' antics. As she listens, she uses the glue to attach the leaf to her paper. She interrupts him to tell him that she is making a butterfly garden and that it has fifty butterflies in it.

From the moment they pick up their first crayon, children are enchanted with art materials. Art is such a joyful part of early childhood curriculum that it is easy to overlook the many developmental and learning purposes it serves. Open-ended art experiences give children the freedom to explore and express their creativity using a variety of materials and mediums. For young children, the process is much more important than the final product. It takes a lot of scribbling to be able to make more deliberate marks on paper, which then leads to more recognizable shapes and, finally, to recognizable objects, letters, and numbers. These stages are directly related to children's growing cognitive understanding that the marks we make on paper have meaning and can be symbols that represent our thinking in objects and, ultimately, words.

Open-ended art experiences are different from crafts. While crafts can have beneficial value, such as making community-helper hats or animal puppets that the children can use for dramatic play, open-ended art experiences truly provide foundational opportunities for creativity and intellectual development. Examples of open-ended art include coloring with markers or crayons, easel painting, fingerpainting, watercoloring, sponge painting, painting with different utensils, or collage-making. Provide a blank canvas and see what develops.

INVITING CHILDREN TO ENGAGE IN OPEN-ENDED ART

The key to engaging children in open-ended art experiences is to provide variety in utensils and surfaces. For painting, you can offer different combinations of colors and types of paper, a variety of surfaces, different colors and textures of paint, lots of containers to hold paint, and interesting utensils. For example, one day children might find red construction paper, egg cartons filled with paint, and cotton swabs on a table inviting them to explore. Another day, it might be newsprint, paint in fruit cups from the recycling bin, and toothbrushes. Opportunities for open-ended art in the form of making collages or sculptures can come from collections of loose parts and recycled materials for the children to explore. A well-stocked shelf full of art supplies allows for creativity and discovery.

OPEN-ENDED ART EXPERIENCES SUPPORT LEARNING ACROSS DOMAINS

Art experiences provide opportunities for children to enrich their developmental skills across the domains of language and literacy, social and emotional skills, physical skills, and cognitive development while also contributing to their growing understandings of math and science.

As children create with art materials, they have the chance to talk with other children or their teachers about what they are drawing or making and the textures, colors, and shapes they notice, which further enhances their language skills. They often use descriptive language related to their creations. They begin to create their own symbols that represent their thinking, which contributes to their ability to understand literacy symbols.

Drawing, painting, and creating provide opportunities to enhance physical development. Children build fine motor skills when using art tools such as crayons or paintbrushes. They enhance their eye-hand

THE MATHEMATICS OF PAINTING

Types of surfaces × Colors
              × Consistency of paint
              × Objects to paint with
              × Containers to paint from
_____

          = Thousands of unique painting experiences that are
              engaging, open ended, and process oriented!

coordination when figuring out how to get the paint out of a container or getting the right amount on a brush. Gross motor development is promoted when working at an easel or creating a mural on the floor.

When children work together to create a painting or sculpture, their social skills are enriched. They have the chance to help each other collect and use materials. They have opportunities to express their thoughts and emotions through artistic endeavors, nurturing their emotional development.

Art experiences provide opportunities to explore properties of materials such as size, thickness, and texture. When mixing paints or problem-solving how to get the tape to hold the arms on their robot, children are deepening their conceptual understandings about how the world works and furthering their cognitive development. The following lists art materials typically found in preschool classrooms.

- Variety of types and sizes of paper
- Crayons, markers, chalk, and paint
- Scissors, brushes, droppers, tape, and glue
- Collage materials, such as pompoms and fabric scraps
- Sculpture materials, such as cardboard boxes, playdough, and tubes
- Easels, paint smocks, and drying racks

Collect Paper and Surfaces for Drawing and Painting

To attract children's interest in drawing or painting, vary the paper and surfaces you provide. Recycled papers, scraps of cardboard, or discarded junk mail are interesting to children and readily available to teachers. You can also vary the size of the paper or surface to promote interest.

Paper

- Newspaper
- Newsprint
- Construction paper
- Sulfite paper
- Manila paper
- Watercolor paper
- Graph paper
- Notebook paper
- Copy paper
- Recycled stationery
- Pages from wallpaper books
- Pages from phone books
- Exam paper
- Butcher paper
- Chart tablet paper

Lu and Rylan are painting empty plastic 2-liter bottles with tempera paint. They hold the tops of the bottles with one hand while using a brush with their other hand to paint the surfaces, chatting easily while they work. Lu says that she is painting her bottle purple because it is her favorite color. Rylan says he likes lots of colors so he is going to use all of the colors to paint his. They both agree that they can paint their bottles however they want and they will both be pretty. Lu compliments Rylan's bottle by saying that he has done a really super great job, and he returns the compliment. Rylan then observes that it takes a long time to paint these bottles and Lu agrees. Lu adds that some people paint really fast but that she and Rylan do not paint really fast. Again they agree that it is okay for some people to paint fast and some people to not paint fast.

Surfaces

- Paper plates
- Cardboard boxes
- Cardboard scrap pieces
- Poster board
- Recycled food boxes
- Coffee filters
- Paper sacks
- Cardboard tubes
- Plastic bottles
- Aluminum foil
- Paper towels

Tip: Create and print your own graph paper using the table function in a word-processing program.

COLLECT CONTAINERS FOR PAINT

When children get paint from a variety of containers, they have opportunities to refine their fine motor skills. It is a different experience to wipe excess paint from the edge of an egg carton than it is to wipe paint from a muffin tin. It is also more interesting and engaging than simply getting paint from a regular paint cup. The following is a list of ideas for containers to hold paint.

- Butter tubs
- Small paper plates
- Aluminum pie pans
- Small plastic cups
- Molded foil
- Egg cartons
- Muffin tins
- Bottom of a plastic soda bottle
- Recycled bakery containers
- Cookie sheets
- Fruit cups
- Squeeze bottles
- Spray bottles

COLLECT UTENSILS FOR PAINTING

By collecting different gadgets and utensils for painting, teachers can support children's creative expression and conceptual understandings. Variety in utensils creates variety in experiences for children, which enhances the artistic process. The following is a list of ideas for items to use as painting utensils.

- Small watercolor brushes
- Large easel brushes
- Foam brushes
- Roller brushes
- Cotton swabs
- Craft feathers
- Sponges
- Mini sponges
- Fingers, knees, toes
- Toothbrushes
- Blocks
- Baby-doll feet
- Small cups
- Vinyl animal hooves
- Cardboard tubes
- String
- Golf balls
- Cotton balls
- Toy cars
- Fake flowers
- Pipettes
- Bath puffs
- Ice
- Cookie cutters
- Plant parts

Several children are at the art table mixing colors. Their teacher has set up the area by filling an ice cube tray with diluted liquid watercolor paint. The children are practicing using pipettes to suction up the paint and then squeeze out drops onto flattened coffee filters. As the drops hit the filters, they spread out into circular shapes. The children talk as they work, pointing out the circles and how sometimes the colors will mix. Jon lets everyone know that red and blue make purple. Other children try it themselves and are excited to see that they also made purple.

Lint Roller Imprinting

Materials

Recycled lint rollers   Glue

Craft foam   Foam stickers

Scissors

1. Cut out craft foam shapes, and glue them to a recycled lint roller. Or, children can just put foam stickers on the lint roller.

2. Encourage the children to roll the tool in paint and then roll it on another surface such as newsprint.

Paint Rollers

Materials

Cardboard tubes   Small pebbles or other

Hot-glue gun   small objects
    (adult use only)

String

1. Use hot glue to attach string or small objects onto sturdy cardboard tubes.

2. Encourage the children to roll the tubes in paint and make impressions on paper.

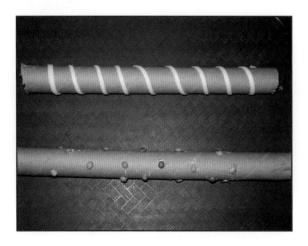

COLLECT ART TOOLS AND CREATE PAINTS_____

Art Tools

- Wavy scissors
- Hole punch
- Rulers
- Tape
- Scissors
- Colored tape

Ideas for Adding Texture to Tempera Paint

- Slimy: add corn syrup
- Gritty: add sand
- Slippery: add powdered gelatin
- Lumpy: add flour

- Shiny: add sugar
- Sparkly: add salt
- Creamy: add liquid starch
- Scented: add flavored gelatin

Salad Spinner Art

Materials

Plastic salad spinner   Thinned tempera paint
Coffee filters or paper   Pipette
Scissors

1. Cut the paper or coffee filter to fit inside the salad spinner.

2. Place the paper inside the spinner.

3. Encourage the children to use a pipette to drip paint onto the paper.

4. Cover and spin!

Liquid Watercolor Paint

Materials

Dried-out, water-based   1 cup hot water per
    markers   color (adult only)
Watercolor paint cakes   Plastic water bottles

1. Pull out the inner felt parts of dried-out markers, or pop out the individual cakes in a name-brand watercolor tray.

2. Fill each bottle with 1 cup of hot water.

3. Drop a color in the water, and allow it to sit overnight. The watercolor cake will dissolve; the marker insert will release the leftover ink.

4. Repeat for each color you wish to make.

As Robert walked in the classroom one morning, he noticed the paint and paper waiting. Three plates holding different colors of paint and several different sizes of cardboard tubes were lined up in the middle of the table. Single sheets of paper waited at every seat. As soon as he had hung his coat and backpack on his cubby hook, he headed straight to the table. His teacher greeted him and then handed him a paint smock, which he quickly pulled over his head. He began experimenting with a tube by dipping an end in the paint and then placing it on his paper, where it left a circle-shaped imprint. After a while, he began using the smaller tubes to make smaller imprints inside the larger imprints. When he finished, he placed his painting on the rack to dry before heading to join his friends in the block area.

Recycled Crayons

Materials

Molds, such as those for candy, soap, ice cubes, or gelatin

Used crayons

Recycled aluminum cans

Pot or large saucepan

Water

Stove (adult use only)

Craft sticks

1. On a stove, heat a pot filled with three inches of water.

2. Remove the paper wrappings from the used crayons, and break the crayons into small pieces.

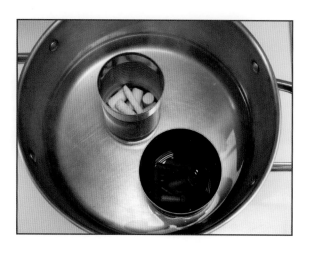

3. Sort the crayons by color, and place each color in an aluminum can.

4. When the water simmers, set the cans in the water.

5. Use crafts sticks to stir the colors frequently. Melt the crayons completely.

6. Pour the colors into molds. If you wish, you can create layered colors by cooling each color, then adding another color on top.

7. Allow the crayons to cool completely before popping them from the molds.

COLLECT MATERIALS FOR MAKING COLLAGES AND SCULPTURES

The opportunity to make collages and sculptures moves children beyond two-dimensional explorations. Prospects for problem solving multiply as children learn that stick glue is not strong enough to hold the seashell to the paper or that the cardboard box they thought to use to make a robot was too small to fulfill their plan. The following lists ideas for items to provide for collages and sculptures.

Collage

Paper scraps	Seeds	Ribbon	Wallpaper scraps
Fabric scraps	Cotton balls	Lace	Pompoms
Coffee filters	Hole-punch dots	Googly eyes	Recycled flyers
Wrapping paper	Tissue paper	Sequins	Adhesive notepads
Yarn scraps	Greeting cards	Cardboard	Paint sample cards
Shells	Confetti	Colored tape	Buttons
Leaves	Aluminum foil	Newspaper	Craft sticks
Dried flowers	Rickrack	Magazines	
Craft feathers	Shredded paper	Felt scraps	

Sculpture

- Cardboard
- Cardboard tubes
- Masking tape
- Chenille stems
- Paper plates
- Small boxes
- Shoe boxes
- Aluminum foil
- Craft sticks
- Beads
- Clothespins
- Wooden shapes
- Paper clips
- Tape
- Brads
- Pie tins
- Recycled boxes and containers

MATERIALS IN ACTION—BODY PARTS

Several children have decided to make robots using materials they found in the sculpture box near the art center. They talk and periodically ask each other and their teacher for help as they work. Penny finds a large box that she says will be the body and a small box for the head. Two potato-chip canisters become the legs. She uses duct tape to attach the body parts, asking the teacher for help on occasion. When the body of her robot is complete, she draws ears and earrings on the side of the head box. Liam admires her work and makes his own robot using hers as a reference. He says his is a boy and draws a simple face on the head box and a belly button on the body.

6 Writing Materials

At their weekly planning meeting, the teachers in the prekindergarten classroom shared their observations of the children's use of the trays of sand they had added to their classroom the previous week. Carol had noticed that many of the children had used it for drawing, but that some had used it for writing their names and other words. Prisha shared a story about a child writing the entire alphabet on a tray. Mark shared his observation of a child writing his name while telling a story about the time his family had gone to the beach and written their names in the sand. The teachers agreed that not only were the children enjoying the sand trays, but they also were benefiting from using them.

Writing and drawing development begin in the same manner: with the exploration of writing utensils. From the first moment toddlers begin scribbling on paper, they are on their way in the wondrous journey that leads to reading and writing. Early random scribbling becomes more controlled and then moves to deliberate mark making. In later preschool, children are able to make more recognizable objects and letter shapes. As scribbling is so important in the progression of writing, support and value these early attempts at understanding how the marks made on paper can be symbols for objects or words. Scribbling means so much more than just random marks. When children are ready, assist in their developing ability to write letters by starting with the letters in their names.

In the classroom, the best literacy activities emerge from the context of other classroom activities. For example, after hearing a story, a child might be inspired to draw the main character and label it. Or after watching the teacher writing everyone's favorite food on a chart, children want to copy it. Children also begin to see the necessity of writing when a classmate is ill and everyone wants to sign the get-well card. The first goal is to provide a supportive environment with a variety of writing materials and encourage children at every step in the process of becoming writers.

INVITING CHILDREN TO ENGAGE IN OPEN-ENDED WRITING

Providing open-ended writing opportunities for preschoolers is the key to supporting children's progression from scribbling to writing. To inspire them to want to write, start with basic writing materials and then add inspiration through variety in paper, writing surfaces, and writing utensils. Even the simplest addition to the writing area can create excitement and enthusiasm in children for writing.

OPEN-ENDED WRITING EXPERIENCES SUPPORT LEARNING ACROSS DOMAINS

Creating opportunities for children to engage with writing materials enhances children's development in many areas. Through their explorations, children can develop language and literacy skills, fine motor skills, social-emotional skills, science and math learning, and cognitive skills.

Opportunities to share their thoughts and spoken words through written symbols and through conversations about their drawings or early writing attempts nurture language and literacy development. Children may ask others for help as they begin to write or spell.

Open-ended writing experiences allow children to strengthen their fine motor skills when drawing or writing on a variety of surfaces. They develop great hand control over time as they practice scribbling and writing.

Activities such as drawing pictures or writing letters to friends and family members strengthen their relationships and further enhance their social-emotional development. Sharing materials or taking turns with others when using literacy tools builds social skills. As they work to draw and write, they develop attention span and focus when using materials.

Cognitive development is enhanced as they build greater understandings of the purposes of written communication and the tools used. Writing experiences provide for deeper exploration of symbols such as letters and numerals. The following lists writing materials typically found in preschool classrooms.

- Variety of types and sizes of paper
- Assortment of writing utensils, such as crayons, markers, and pencils
- Erasable surfaces, such as chalkboards and dry-erase boards
- Stamps and stamp pads
- Finger-sliding trays filled with sand

Finger-sliding trays filled with a shallow of layer of a medium such as salt or sand hold great interest for children. These experiences provide another avenue to support scribbling, drawing, and early writing.

The following lists ideas for items to use and include with finger-sliding trays.

- Plastic trays
- Cookie sheets
- Plastic bins
- Cake pans
- Stove-burner covers
- Shallow cardboard boxes
- Salt
- Shaving cream
- Sand
- Fingerpaint
- Cotton swabs
- Paintbrushes
- Craft sticks
- Craft feathers
- Unsharpened pencils

MATERIALS IN ACTION—NAME WRITING

Isabella sits at the table by herself using a finger-sliding tray full of salt. Her teacher notices that she is attempting to write her own name. Isabella begins in the middle of the tray and writes ISA before running out of room. She then shakes the tray gently back and forth to clear it before beginning again. This time, she starts farther to the left and gets all the way to the second L before running out of room. It takes all of the teacher's willpower not to suggest that she begin closer to the edge of the tray. On Isabella's third attempt, she is able to write her whole name without running out of room. She looks up, sees her teacher watching her, and grins from ear to ear.

Hair Gel Freezer Bag

Materials

Quart-size resealable   Duct tape
  freezer bag   Cardboard scrap
Hair gel

1. Add approximately 1/4 cup of hair gel to a freezer bag.

2. Seal the bag with duct tape.

3. Place the bag on a flat surface, and push the gel toward the center of the bag using your fingertips.

4. Duct tape the edges of the bag for extra durability.

5. Children can use their fingers or a cotton swab to draw and write on the bag.

Optional: Tape the bag onto a scrap of cardboard the size of the bag, and secure the bag using duct tape. This will allow for a flat surface at all times.

COLLECT AND CREATE PAPER TO INSPIRE WRITING

To inspire children to draw and write, provide a variety of paper types that you have collected or created. When children frequently find new materials to write on, they are encouraged to begin.

The following is a list of ideas for writing materials.

- Old calendar pages
- Spiral notebooks
- File folders
- Adhesive notepads
- Note cards
- Sheet music

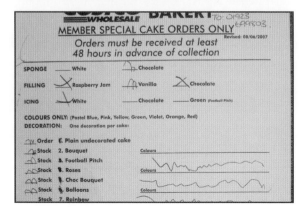

Since it was spring, the preschool class had been planting seeds and exploring various types of plants. The teachers had added flower stationery to the writing center. Raquel and Yui were excited to find them in a basket on the shelf. They sorted through all of the sheets until they each decided on the same one with a photo of pink roses. Raquel grabbed the holder of colored pencils and took it to a table, where both girls began "writing letters." Raquel said she was writing a letter to her mom. Yui started on her stationery but then got up to search the baskets on the shelf for some envelopes.

- Notebook paper
- Construction paper
- Textured paper
- Recycled paper

- Poster-board scraps
- Card stock
- Order forms
- Greeting cards

- Thank-you notes
- Newsprint
- Sentence-strip paper
- Index cards

- Adding-machine tape
- Envelopes

CREATE PAPER MATERIALS FOR WRITING

In addition to collecting interesting paper, you can create items to interest the children in writing.

- Cards: prefold card stock
- Paper books: fold and staple sheets together
- Graph paper: use the table function in your word-processing program
- Stationery: use the border function in your word-processing program
- Grocery lists
- To-do lists
- Theme-shaped paper

COLLECT AND CREATE WRITING UTENSILS_____

Providing a variety of writing utensils inspires children to want to write. Start by providing crayons, markers, and pencils of different types. Novelty pencils or pens decorated with feathers or flowers will often be the most popular items on the shelf. The following is a list of ideas for writing utensils.

▮ Thin and thick crayons

▮ Fine- and wide-tipped markers

▮ Multicultural crayons and markers

▮ Metallic crayons

▮ Scented markers

▮ Pens

▮ Gel pens

▮ Highlighters

▮ Thin and thick pencils

▮ Colored pencils

▮ Pencil toppers, such as flowers and feathers

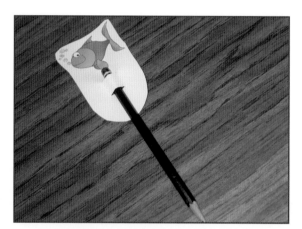

Craft Foam Toppers

Materials
Craft foam
Scissors
Pens or pencils

1. Cut out a variety of shapes from craft foam.

2. In each shape, cut a half-inch horizontal slit.

3. Insert the pen or pencil.

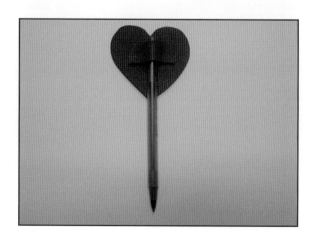

Michael is walking around the classroom with a clipboard and the feather pen from the writing center. One of his teachers notices that he is making frequent stops to jot on the clipboard. As he passes her, she comments, "I see you've got the clipboard." He responds, "Yeah, I just need to check on a few things." He moves on and continues for another five minutes or so. After he has abandoned the clipboard to move on to something else, the teacher looks at the paper. She notices that the page is full of scribbled lines and letter-like shapes. She also finds the letters of Michael's name across the bottom of the page.

Collect and Create Erasable Writing Surfaces

Many classrooms have erasable surfaces such as dry-erase or magnetic boards where children may practice their drawing and writing skills, but you can create your own to provide more variety in writing experiences. For example, let the children write and draw with markers on disposable plastic plates. Laminate sentence-strip paper, and encourage the children to use dry-erase markers to write on it. Make your own dry-erase boards by purchasing shower board at your local home-improvement store and asking them to cut it to the sizes you want.

Dry-Erase Cube

Materials

Small box	Colored tape, such as
Dry-erase	washi tape
contact paper	Dry-erase markers

1. Cover a small box with dry-erase contact paper.

2. Cover the edges with colored tape for durability.

3. Encourage the children to write and draw on the cube.

Sonja is using a dry-erase marker to draw on a disposable plastic plate. She has a dry washcloth to wipe it clean waiting nearby. At first she scribbles on the plate in a random manner. After the surface starts to fill up, she begins coloring in a section at a time. Once the plate is completely covered, she stops and then wipes it clean with the washcloth. It takes her a while to get all of the markings erased. She then draws spiral shapes around the edges and into the middle of the plate. After she uses the washcloth to erase it again, she leaves the table and moves on to another activity.

Cardboard Chalkboard

Materials

Cardboard

Scissors

Chalkboard contact paper

Colored tape, such as washi tape

Chalk

1. Cut a square from the cardboard.

2. Cover the cardboard square with chalkboard contact paper.

3. Tape the edges for durability.

4. Encourage the children to write and draw on the chalkboard.

COLLECT AND CREATE WRITING TOOLS AND INSPIRATIONS FOR WRITING

In addition to providing great variety in writing surfaces and utensils, you can also provide other literacy props and inspirations to promote writing development in children. Office supplies such as tape dispensers and staplers are appealing to children. Once they have stapled the paper, children often want to write on it. Other writing inspirations, such as garage-sale dots or foil stars, can be placed near paper to see what engages the children's interests. The following is a list of ideas of items to encourage writing.

▦ Clipboards	▦ Masking tape	▦ Paper clips	▦ Hole punches
▦ Clear tape	▦ Decorative tape	▦ Novelty paper clips	▦ Rubber bands

- Staplers
- Rulers
- Scissors
- Googly eyes
- Foil sticker stars
- Foam shapes
- Stickers
- Hole protectors
- Colored sticker dots
- Adhesive letters
- Letter stamps

Copy Cubes

Materials

Foam dice
White card stock
Permanent marker
Scissors

Hot-glue gun
  (adult use only)
Painter's tape

1. Cut six pieces of card stock to the size of the sides for each die.

2. Draw patterns and shapes on each piece of card stock.

3. Attach the card stock to the sides of the die with hot glue.

4. Cover the edges of the cube with painter's tape.

5. Encourage the children to copy the shapes, lines, and squiggles they see on the cube.

William and Rashaad were working at the table near the writing center with the stapler and magazines. They were taking turns stapling several torn sheets together. Eventually, the stapler ran out of staples, but the boys were unsure of what was wrong. William kept trying to make the tool staple while saying that it wasn't working. Rashaad was the first to suggest that maybe it was empty. William called out to the teacher for more staples. She brought more to them and asked if they needed any help. William insisted he could do it himself but struggled to figure out how to refill the stapler. Rashaad said he knew how and prompted William on each step. With Rashaad's help, William was able to refill the stapler, and the boys then went back to stapling the magazines.

CREATE MATERIALS FOR STAMPING AND RUBBING

Children are interested in stamps and stamp pads. They often begin exploring by just stamping to see what happens. Soon, they move on to stamping the letters of their names and then stamping the letters of the names of their family members and friends. You can create stamping materials to encourage the children to explore letters.

Alphabet Block Stamps

Materials

Wooden alphabet blocks Tempera paint
Chenille stems Paper plate
Hot-glue gun (adult use only) Paper

1. Shape chenille stems to create letters that will fit on the side of a wooden block.

2. Attach the letter to the block using hot glue. **Tip:** When creating letter stamps, be sure to attach the letter backwards. As children stamp, the letter will be correctly positioned on the paper.

3. Encourage the children to dip a stamp into the paint and to use it to make an impression on the paper.

Letter and Shape Rubbing Cards

Materials

Card stock or cardboard scraps

Hot-glue gun (adult use only)

Permanent marker

Scissors

Crayons with wrappers removed

Paper

1. Cut card stock or cardboard scraps into squares of the size you desire.

2. Draw a shape, letter, or numeral on each square with a permanent marker. You can focus on letters or numerals you are teaching the children, or you can create themed images.

3. Trace the shape with hot glue and allow to cool.

4. Children can place paper over the pieces and rub using crayons.

Letter Stamps

Materials

Foam letters

26 foam puzzle pieces, wooden blocks, polystyrene cubes, sponges, or cardboard scraps

Hot-glue gun (adult use only)

Paper

Tempera paint

Paper plate

1. Using foam letters, hot glue a letter to a cardboard scrap, polystyrene cube, sponge, wooden block, or large foam puzzle piece. **Tip:** Place the letter backward so that it will appear correctly when stamped.

2. Encourage the children to dip the stamps into the paint and use them to create impressions on the paper.

MATERIALS IN ACTION—NAMING LETTERS

Stamps made from foam alphabet puzzle pieces and stamp pads are set up on the table. Becky and Julissa are finding the letters in their own names and stamping them on paper. Becky suggests they do each other's names. They work together to find the right letters. Julissa points out that her name is longer and has more letters than Becky's. Becky agrees.

7 Playdough and Tools

Taryn had recently learned to write her name and was having fun writing it everywhere. She wrote it on the dry-erase board, with paint at the easel, in the sand in the sensory table, and even shaped chenille stems into the letters of her name. One of her teachers asked her where she was going to write her name next. She thought for a minute and then decided she would write it with playdough. She

asked the teacher if she could use the alphabet playdough mats. Taryn sorted through the mats and found the letters in her name. After she was finished rolling "snakes" to make letters, she asked the teacher to take a picture of her so that she could show her mother.

Playdough is one of those learning materials that children enjoy time and time again. Beyond the fun and sensory satisfaction that children have when they interact with playdough, they also have the

126

opportunity to create and express themselves. Playdough is typically a social activity that offers chances to share, take turns, wait for a turn, and negotiate for the most interesting tool. All of this leads to conversation. When children play together, the desire to communicate drives their language development. Teachers join in, giving names to concepts being developed, such as size, shape, smoothness, flatness, rolling, cutting, or dividing the playdough ball in half. There is no doubt the children are giving their fine motor muscles a workout as they pound, flatten, roll, pull, and poke. They are also expanding their cognitive ability to think abstractly as they imagine that the round, flat piece of dough is a cookie, or that the balls of graduating sizes are a snowman. At each developmental stage, playing with playdough is fun and learning—all rolled together.

INVITING CHILDREN TO EXPLORE PLAYDOUGH

You can make your own cooked playdough so that the children can choose from a variety of colors and scents. Manipulation tools for playdough can include cookie cutters; rolling pins; plastic pizza cutters; cups; tubs; and natural items such as shells, rocks, or twigs. Provide mats or trays and a variety of containers to hold tools—the children will find it difficult to resist the chance to explore all that they can do.

PLAYDOUGH EXPERIENCES SUPPORT LEARNING ACROSS DOMAINS

Playdough experiences support children's learning across the domains of language and literacy development, fine motor development, social and emotional development, science, math, and cognitive development.

Language and literacy development is supported when children talk and have conversations about what they are doing and making with the playdough. They might name the utensils they are using or talk about the representations they are creating. As they describe and explain, they will use new vocabulary and specific concept terms.

MATERIALS IN ACTION—SYMBOLIC REPRESENTATION

Amidst the bakery props in the dramatic-play center of the classroom, Hannah discovers a mini muffin pan and foil muffin cups. She takes them to the table where the blue playdough is set out and announces that she is going to make cupcakes. She separates the foil cups and places one in each cup of the pan. She begins filling them by pulling small pieces of playdough off the larger mound and smashing them down in the cups. She works diligently to make sure that each is filled to the top. When she finishes, she finds several plastic plates from the dramatic play area and places as many cupcakes as will fit on each one. She then walks around the room asking her friends if they would like a cupcake.

Ralph and Tino are at the table with the brown playdough and toy dinosaurs. They have made irregular mounds with the dough and are placing the dinosaurs in them. They talk back and forth, make their dinosaurs roar, and pretend to chase each other. Tino uses one of the dinosaurs to make tracks in the dough. He tells Ralph that these are like the real dinosaurs that get their feet in the mud and that in a billion thousand years archaeologists will find them. Ralph imitates Tino and uses his dinosaur to make tracks.

When rolling, pounding, and pinching the playdough, children have the opportunity to enhance their fine motor muscle strength. As they create sculptures and place objects in playdough, they are building eye-hand coordination. Playdough experiences are often social events, and children have the chance to engage with friends as they take turns, share materials, and solve social conflicts. This also gives them the opportunity to express themselves creatively.

Emerging concepts such as round or flat, long or short, and lumpy or smooth are supported through engaging with playdough and assorted props. Cognitive development is supported through opportunities to problem solve through trial and error. These experiences also enhance understanding of mathematical concepts such as more and less and part and whole as they manipulate the playdough.

The following lists playdough materials typically found in preschool classrooms.

- Variety of colors, scents, and textures
- Tools such as rolling pins, cookie cutters, and scissors
- Loose parts such as beads and buttons
- Natural materials such as rocks and twigs
- Mats, containers, and trays

Create Playdough

Materials

3 cups flour

1 1/2 cups salt

3 tablespoons vegetable oil

2 tablespoons cream of tartar

3 cups water

Optional: food coloring or liquid watercolor, extracts such as lemon or vanilla, and drink-mix packets for both color and scent

1. Combine the dry ingredients in a large pot.

2. Add the wet ingredients to the dry ingredients, and stir well.

3. Begin cooking over low heat, stirring continually. If you wish, add scent or color to the playdough.

4. When the playdough thickens, remove it from the heat and turn it out onto a cutting board.

5. Knead the playdough when it cools.

6. Store it in an air-tight container.

COLLECT TOOLS FOR USE WITH PLAYDOUGH

From cutting to pounding to imprinting, tools matter when it comes to playdough. A quick search in the kitchen or recycling bin will yield a multitude of possibilities.

- Whisks
- Combs and brushes
- Potato masher
- Craft sticks
- Rolling pins
- Cookie cutters
- Plastic utensils
- Paper plates
- Scissors
- Mason-jar lids
- Toy tools
- Muffin tins
- Toy animals
- Interlocking blocks
- Plastic curlers
- Rubber stamps
- Letter imprinters
- Nuts and bolts

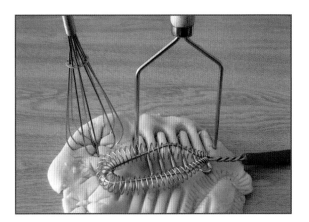

COLLECT MATERIALS FOR USE WITH PLAYDOUGH

Adding loose parts such as the following to playdough will promote dramatic play and problem solving.

- Straws
- Jewels
- Chenille stems
- Pony beads
- Toothpicks
- Coffee stir sticks
- Googly eyes
- Poker chips
- Marbles
- Decorative tiles
- PVC pipe
- Golf tees
- Food-pouch caps
- Outlet covers
- Buttons
- Artificial flowers
- Craft feathers
- Seashells
- Sticks
- Twigs
- Leaves
- Rocks
- Tree cookies

Red playdough sits on a table next to a half-dozen egg carton full of acorns, pebbles, and pony beads. Each section of the egg carton holds a different type of item. Several laminated mats have been placed around the table. Peter sits down at one of them and begins making a mound of playdough, which he flattens into a circular shape. Next, he places one color of pony bead all the way around the edge of his mound. Then he chooses pebbles and begins placing those around the mound right above the previously placed beads. He begins a third round with another color of pony bead before leaving the table when a friend calls him over to play in the block area.

COLLECT AND CREATE MATS AND TRAYS FOR PLAYDOUGH

Providing mats and trays for playdough creates individual spaces for exploration and can entice children to explore.

- Restaurant serving trays
- Cookie sheets
- Cutting boards
- Vinyl placemats

You also can create simple activity mats using children's artwork or laminated images.

Letter or Numeral Activity Mat

Materials

Paper place mats
Construction paper
Scissors
Pencil
Clear contact paper

1. Trace letters or numerals on the construction paper, and cut them out.

2. Place a letter or numeral on a paper place mat.

3. Cover the mat with clear contact paper or laminate it for durability.

4. Continue until you have made a mat for each letter of the alphabet or each numeral you are teaching.

5. Encourage the children to shape playdough to match the letter or numeral on the mat.

Face Mats

Materials

Paper place mats   Construction paper

Scissors   Pencil

Clear contact paper

1. Trace the outlines of faces on the construction paper.

2. Cut them out, and place a face on each place mat.

3. Cover each mat with clear contact paper or laminate it for durability.

4. Encourage the children to create facial features on the mats using the playdough.

Playdough Cake Mat

Materials

Paper place mats   Pencil

Construction paper   Clear contact paper

Scissors

1. Trace a cake shape on the construction paper.

2. Cut it out, and place the cake on a place mat.

3. Cover each mat with clear contact paper or laminate it for durability.

4. Encourage the children to decorate the cakes using playdough flowers, candles, and so on.

Playdough Fish Pond

Materials

Blue or green   Pencil
  butter paper   Clear contact paper
Scissors

1. Trace a pond shape on the butcher paper.

2. Cut out the pond shape, and cover it with clear contact paper or laminate it for durability.

3. Encourage the children to use playdough to make fish, frogs, and other animals to live in the pond.

MATERIALS IN ACTION—
ONE-TO-ONE CORRESPONDENCE

There are green playdough and twigs on the table after outdoor time. After washing her hands, Serena chooses a mat and grabs a handful of dough from the bag. She begins by kneading and mashing the playdough. Eventually, she begins rolling small ball shapes. After she has several lined up, she pokes a single twig upright in each one. By this time, other children have joined her, and they chat easily. She continues making balls and placing twigs. Alice mimics her actions and adds that she is making birthday candles. Serena removes her twigs, gathers the smaller balls into a larger one, flattens it, and places the twigs around the perimeter. She tells Alice that she made a birthday cake.

8

Science Materials

Mrs. Whatley had created a pendulum using PVC pipe, and it was a big hit with the children. It was originally set up with supporting props for stacking (and knocking down) such as foam blocks, recycled plastic cups, and small cardboard boxes. By the end of the week, the children were pulling materials from all over the classroom to see how they would work. Their teacher had purposefully provided minimal support on how to use the pendulum, and she was delighted to see how the children's understandings of how it worked progressed during the week. At first, most of the children threw the ball at the stacks to knock them down, but quickly they understood that they could pull back and swing the ball with the same effect. Shortly thereafter, many of the children figured out how to position themselves so that they could swing the ball at the appropriate angle to achieve maximum impact.

Science learning opportunities are everywhere. We often think of science as a very narrow subject, but the reality is that many of the activities that drive young children's curiosity build on their emerging scientific understandings. Children are little scientists, constantly trying to figure out the world. Even what seem to be simple activities, such as racing cars down block ramps, mixing paints at the easel, testing magnets, looking at shells and feathers through a magnifying glass, or watching and waiting for a seed to sprout in the gardening bin, assist children in developing their knowledge about processes and concepts such as gravity, motion, matter, change, and growth. Some of the most meaningful scientific learning experiences occur spontaneously when a child notices something that interests her and she begins to explore. Take advantage of these moments because natural curiosity drives and motivates learning. Build on this natural curiosity by introducing photos, nonfiction books, and real items from nature to entice children to explore, question, and think. Actively manipulating materials helps children build the foundation for deeper and more complex firsthand knowledge of how the world works.

Inviting Children to Explore with Science Materials

Spark children's interest in science explorations by frequently rotating materials on the science shelf. You can also set up tabletop explorations; for example, placing a balance scale in the center of a small table surrounded by rocks and pebbles is an invitation to see how many rocks can be placed on each side. Setting a couple of rulers out with some toy animals is an invitation to measure and compare lengths and heights. A magnifier with a collection of seashells on a tray is an invitation to look at the details.

Exploring Science Materials Supports Learning across Domains

While playing with materials, children have opportunities to enhance their skills in multiple ways. Science materials can support language and literacy development, fine and gross motor development, socio-emotional development, and cognitive development.

As children engage with science materials, they have conversations about their discoveries with other children and teachers, which enhance their language development and give them the opportunity to use new vocabulary and scientific terminology. They can explore letters and numerals on science materials, tools, and images within their environment.

Engaging with science tools such as tongs and pipettes provides opportunities for children to enhance their eye-hand coordination. They also have opportunities to build gross motor skills by coordinating their actions to swing a pendulum or shine a flashlight.

When children explore science materials together, they have opportunities to build their social and emotional skills. Relationships are strengthened through working with others or sharing excitement over a discovery. When children are focused on interesting materials, they maintain and build their attention spans.

Children have many opportunities for cognitive growth through exploration of science materials. They are able to build on their concepts related to scientific knowledge such as gravity or force. Opportunities to weigh and measure materials increase their understandings of math concepts. Science materials provide opportunities to solve problems through exploration and trial and error.

SCIENCE MATERIALS TYPICALLY FOUND IN PRESCHOOL CLASSROOMS_____

Many preschool classrooms have a designated area or center for science exploration, but you can encourage investigations all around the classroom as well as outside. You can provide tools such as magnifying glasses, color paddles, magnets, rulers, and tongs; natural items such as leaves, rocks, shells, and bird's nests; balance scales and materials to weigh; and clipboards, notebooks, and writing utensils to record discoveries. The following is a list of ideas for science explorations.

- Seashells
- Pinecones
- Leaves
- Grass
- Hay
- Empty wasp nests
- Feathers
- Rocks and pebbles
- Fossils
- Streamers
- Birds' nests

- Items to test for floating or sinking
- Noisemakers
- Sticks
- Twigs
- Bark
- Tree cookies
- Driftwood
- Sand
- Soils
- Sawdust
- Raw cotton or wool

- Gourds
- Acorns

- Seeds
- Beans

MATERIALS IN ACTION—COMPARING LENGTH

Cardboard tubes cut into a variety of lengths rest on the table, along with several plastic 12-inch rulers. Jon, Beth, and Samson jump right in and start measuring. Their conversation centers on which tubes are longer, which are shorter, and the lengths of the tubes as determined by their measurement with the rulers. Beth seems to know more about how to measure with a ruler and is careful to line the tool up precisely with the tube before reporting the number. Jon tends to hold the ruler next to the tube and then report a number without looking at it. Samson watches Beth and imitates her precise actions but still seems to guess at the numbers he is reporting. Beth then has the idea to line up the tubes from biggest to smallest. The other two children follow her lead.

Thrifty Teacher's Guide to Creative Learning Centers

Offer a variety of tools, such as the following:

- Scales
- Magnifying glasses
- Magnets or magnetic wands
- Prisms
- Shatterproof mirrors
- Plastic, blunt-tip tweezers or tongs
- Pipettes
- Sand timers
- Flashlights
- Plastic hand air pump
- Bulb or medical syringes
- Nonfiction books
- Writing materials
- Clipboards
- Woodworking tools
- Rulers or measuring tape

COLLECT AND CREATE MATERIALS FOR SCIENCE EXPLORATION

Clothespin Catapult

Materials

Small boxes or wooden boards
Clothespin
Craft stick
Recycled bottle caps
Pompoms
Hot-glue gun (adult use only)

1. Use hot glue to attach the clothespin to a box or board.

2. Attach the craft stick to the top of the clothespin to add length.

3. Glue the bottle cap to the end of the craft stick, leaving finger space at the end.

4. Children can place a pompom in the cap and activate the catapult by gently pressing down and releasing the end of the craft stick near the cap.

Texture Boards

Materials

Cutting boards

Assorted fabric and textile scraps

Hot-glue gun (adult use only)

1. Cut squares from the fabric and textile scraps.

2. Attach them to the cutting board using hot glue.

3. Encourage the children to explore and describe the textures.

Magnifier Block

Materials

Wooden stacking game pieces	Hot-glue gun (adult use only)
Magnifier sheets	Wood glue (optional)

1. Create two identical wooden frames by using hot glue to connect four wooden blocks.

2. Cut a square from the magnifier sheet in dimensions a little smaller than the frame.

3. Use hot glue to attach the magnifier sheet to one frame, and then attach the other frame so that the magnifier sheet is sandwiched between the two frames.

Optional: Use wood glue to fill in seams for added durability.

Cardboard Catapult

Materials

2 sturdy cardboard tubes	Duct tape
Recycled fruit cup	Hot-glue gun (adult use only)
Pompoms	Cylinder unit block

1. Use hot glue to attach the cardboard tubes together, end to end.

2. Wrap the joints with duct tape for added stability.

3. Glue a fruit cup to one end.

4. Set the catapult on a cylinder block laid on its side.

5. Children can place pompoms in the fruit cup and then activate the catapult by pressing or stepping on the opposite end.

Cardboard Tubes for Measuring
Materials

Cardboard tubes of varying lengths	Scissors
	Glue
Decorative paper	Rulers

1. Cover the tubes with decorative paper.

2. Provide rulers and encourage the children to measure the tubes and compare their measurements.

PVC Pendulum
Materials

15 feet of 1-inch PVC pipe	2 small carabiner hooks
	Chain
6 1-inch PVC elbows	Utility knife
2 1-inch PVC tee sockets	(adult use only)
PVC pipe cutter	Cardboard brick blocks,
Tennis ball	foam blocks, plastic
Metal molly	cups, or other items
Eye hook	for stacking

1. Cut nine pieces of PVC pipe so that each measures 15 inches long. **Tip:** If you do not have a pipe cutter, the pieces can be cut by an employee at the home improvement store for a nominal fee.

2. Create a frame using the elbows and tees. Leave these unglued for easy storage.

3. Cut a small slit in the tennis ball with the utility knife.

4. Slide a metal molly through the opening.

5. Screw an eye hook into the molly.

6. Attach a chain to the eye hook using a carabiner hook.

7. Wrap the chain around the top of the PVC frame, and adjust the length using the remaining carabiner hook.

8. Encourage the children to stack materials and swing the pendulum.

Variation: Instead of using a chain and tennis ball, cut one leg from panty hose or tights and place a tennis ball inside. Tie the hose to the top of the PVC frame.

Several children are playing together at the table where a pendulum made from PVC pipe is sitting. A variety of stacking materials is available, such as small plastic cups and foam blocks. After some negotiation to determine whose turn it is, Sherri has a chance. The other children stack the blocks for her. After she successfully swings the ball and makes the blocks fly, everyone begins running around and grabbing them so that they can be stacked again. More negotiation ensues to determine who will have the next turn.

Resin Viewers

Materials

Resin kit	Object for viewing, such
Plastic mold or tub	as a shell, a (dead)
Scissors	insect, or a leaf
Craft stick or toothpick	

1. Resin kits can be purchased from a craft store. Follow the manufacturer's instructions when mixing the ingredients. To begin, mix only enough resin to fill your container one-third full.

2. Place your object on top of the resin, and let it sit for two hours.

3. Use a toothpick or craft stick to spread the insect body parts into the position of your choosing, and allow the container to sit overnight.

4. Mix more resin, and fill your container to the desired level. Let the resin sit overnight again.

5. Remove the hardened resin from the container. It may be necessary to cut the container from your finished piece.

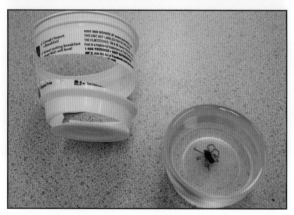

COLLECT AND CREATE MATERIALS FOR EXPLORING WITH MAGNETS_____

Magnets are fascinating to young children. Provide magnets and a variety of materials for the children to explore. Is it magnetic? Encourage them to find out.

- Screws
- Nails
- Pipe fittings
- Metal rings
- Wooden rings
- Nuts and bolts
- Paper clips
- Corks
- Plastic tiles

- Wooden tiles
- Chenille stems
- Twist ties
- Craft sticks
- Toothpicks
- Fabric scraps
- Paper scraps
- Pencils

Magnetic Jars

Materials
Recycled plastic jars
Hot-glue gun (adult use only)
Chenille stems or small metal objects
Magnetic wand

1. If using chenille stems, cut them into small pieces.

2. Place the magnetic objects in the plastic jar.

3. Hot glue the lid closed.

4. Encourage the children to run the magnetic wand around the sides and top of the jar to attract the metallic objects.

Magnetic Fishing

Materials

Construction paper

Scissors

Pencil

Packing tape

Paper clips

Magnetic fishing pole

Blue poster board or fabric

1. Draw and cut out images of fish. Laminate or cover them with packing tape for durability.

2. Attach a paper clip to each fish, and cover with packing tape.

3. Cut a pond shape from blue poster board or fabric.

4. Encourage the children to fish using the magnetic fishing pole.

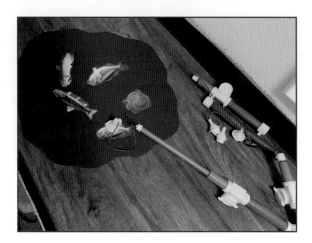

Magnetic Roadway

Materials

Cardboard box

Colored paper

Utility knife (adult use only)

Clear contact paper

Metal car (or hot glue a magnet to the bottom of a plastic car)

Magnetic wand or other magnet

1. Cut the box to resemble a table, using the utility knife.

2. Decorate the box to resemble roadways by gluing paper to the top.

3. Cover the top with contact paper for easy sliding.

4. Children can place a car on the roadway and manipulate the car by sliding a magnet underneath.

A tub on the science shelf holds a variety of small loose parts, including screws, paper clips, washers, corks, plastic tiles, and chenille stems. Several magnetic wands sit next to it. Bobby asks Samir if he wants to play magnets with him. They take the items to the table where they begin trying to pick up the objects with the wands. As they work, they comment on the magnetic properties of the objects. "Corks aren't metal so they don't work." "This is metal. See? It picks up." "The red things don't work. That's because they're plastic. Remember, plastic doesn't magnet." "Chenille stems work because they have metal inside. Look! I got a whole bunch at the same time." "Your magnet is really strong. It can hold it because it's really strong."

COLLECT MATERIALS TO WEIGH AND BALANCE

Provide balance scales and weight scales for the children to explore. They will enjoy weighing and balancing all sorts of items, such as the following.

- Tree cookies
- Pinecones
- Wood chips
- Twigs
- Rocks
- Gourds
- Pebbles
- Cars
- Shells
- Blocks
- Beans
- Counting bears
- Poker chips
- Manipulatives
- Food-pouch caps
- Clothespins
- Decorative beads

Before the children arrive for the day, Mr. Blackmon sets the balance scale on a table near the science area and adds several containers of loose parts—shells, small rocks, pebbles, acorns, and twigs. Throughout the morning, the children visit the scales frequently. Irene makes her way to the table at a time when everyone else is engaged in other activities. She spends a long time simply filling and emptying the buckets with the materials available. Sometimes she sorts the objects and places only one type in the buckets. More often, she combines them. As soon as one side of the scale tips down, she starts adding to the other side. She continues her explorations until it is time to get ready for lunch.

Hanger Scale

Materials

Plastic clothes hanger

Yarn

Scissors

Ruler

Recycled fruit cups

Hole punch

Assorted materials to weigh

1. Punch three holes at equal distances around the top of each fruit cup.

2. Tie an 8-inch piece of yarn to each hole and then pull up and tie a knot so that the cup will hang.

3. Tie a longer piece of yarn to the knot. Repeat for the other cup.

4. Tie each hanging cup to the clothes hanger, ensuring that the cups hang at the same level.

5. Hang the scale from a doorknob or other surface.

6. Children can use materials to try to balance the scale.

CREATE MATERIALS TO EXPLORE LIGHT AND MIRRORS_____

Light, shadow, and reflections engage children's imaginations and inspire rich discussion. Provide materials to encourage them to explore the properties of light.

Shadow Boxes

Materials

Recycled cardboard box | Flashlight
White paper | Scissors
Toy animals | Glue

1. Glue white paper to the insides of the box.

2. Encourage the children to turn the box on its side and place animals in it. They can then shine a flashlight to create shadows.

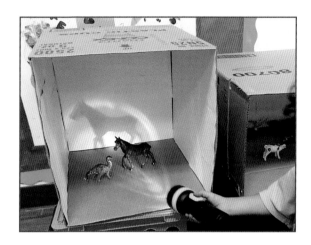

Signal Lights

Materials

Paper-towel tubes | Duct tape
Black tri-fold project | Glue
  display board | Scissors
Black craft foam | Small flashlights
Plastic sandwich bags

1. Cut small shapes from the black craft foam.

2. Cut a 4" x 4" piece of plastic from a sandwich bag.

3. Glue the shapes in the center of the square of plastic.

4. Wrap the plastic over the end of a tube, and secure it with duct tape.

5. Encourage the children to shine a flashlight through the opposite end of the tube to create shadows on the black tri-fold project display stand or other surfaces.

Symmetry Halves

Materials

Symmetrical images,
    such as faces,
    butterflies, circles,
    and hearts

Scissors
Shatterproof mirrors
Clear contact paper

1. Cut the images in half.

2. Cover them with clear contact paper or laminate them.

3. Encourage the children to hold the halved images next to a mirror so that the reflection creates the whole image.

Variation: Provide other items, such as arch blocks, pompoms, rocks, gems, and leaves, for the children to explore with mirrors.

Three-Sided Mirror

Materials

Cardboard box
Utility knife
    (adult use only)
Duct tape

Acrylic mirrors
Hot-glue gun
    (adult use only)

1. Cut the box to create a three-sided base.

2. Cover the outside with duct tape for strength.

3. Cut the acrylic mirrors to fit the box sides by scoring the mirrors with a utility knife and snapping them apart.

4. Attach the mirrors to the three box sides with hot glue.

5. Encourage the children to explore all sorts of items on the three-sided mirror.

9 Sensory Materials

When Sara arrived in the classroom on Monday morning, she was excited to find red water in the sensory table. She had enjoyed the green water that had been in the bin the previous week and had spent time every day exploring it with the funnels. Her teachers decided to use the water and

funnel mixture again because they noticed that the children were still interested in them. This time, they made some small adjustments by changing the color of the water and switching the bowls with measuring cups. Sara jumped right in and invited friends to play with her.

A favorite activity for teachers and children alike is pouring and scooping at the sensory table. While digging into whatever messy material is in the bin on a particular week is extremely fun, it is also a learning experience extraordinaire. Sensory activities promote cognitive and mathematical skills such as concept development (more/less, full/empty), cause and effect, measuring (part to whole), comparison, exploration, problem solving, and spatial awareness. Sensory activities also promote physical skills and fine motor control ranging from eye-hand coordination to an overall coordination of actions. In addition, sensory activities promote social-emotional skills such as sharing and turn taking, cooperation, self-help skills, social problem solving, self-regulation, and attention. Children can only learn so much by watching and being told; they literally need to dig in to gain this knowledge firsthand. At the sensory table, children discover that it takes three small scoops of water to fill up the bucket. They discover that when both the larger scoop and the smaller scoop are full of sand, the larger one is heavier. When teachers interact with children at the sensory table, they point out concepts such as full, empty, heavy, or light. Whether children play alone or with their friends, sensory materials provide a multitude of learning opportunities.

Inviting Children to Explore Sensory Materials

Support children's learning at the sensory table by regularly changing the materials and the utensils. Water from the tap and sand from the playground are the least expensive materials to add, but children also enjoy and learn from other materials such as shredded paper, birdseed (the kind without capsaicin), water beads, or pebbles. You can collect simple materials to use as utensils in the sensory table, such as laundry-soap caps for scooping or recycled yogurt containers for filling. Observe the children's activities to help you decide when to continue with materials or when to change them for something new. You can also use materials related to curriculum concepts. For example, a unit on birds might inspire you to put birdseed in the sensory table or to make a birdseed sensory bottle.

Sensory Materials Support Learning across the Domains

Engaging with sensory materials or playing in a sensory table contribute to children's learning in many areas and promote language and literacy development, physical development, social-emotional development, math and science learning, and cognitive development.

Sensory explorations contribute to children's language and literacy development when children have conversations while playing at a sensory table or exploring sensory bottles. They might use specific vocabulary related to what they are discovering. Sensory materials that incorporate letters or numbers support children's growing understandings of literacy and numeracy.

When children scoop materials or manipulate with tongs, they are enhancing their fine motor skills. Similarly, they are learning to coordinate their actions when they try to pour materials through a funnel into a bottle or cup. Sensory explorations can also promote gross motor skills when children participate in activities such as moving material from a sensory table to a bucket or using a multilevel sand apparatus.

Sensory play enhances social skills when children cooperate with one another and negotiate for favorite tools. It can enhance emotional development by allowing them to express feelings and reduce stress through pleasant sensations. Prolonged engagement with materials can build attention span.

Opportunities to promote cognitive development can be seen in sensory play. Children build conceptual understandings about how the world works, such as how different materials slide through a funnel or what happens when a container is overfilled. They also have the chance to create and solve their own problems, such as when they try to determine which size scoop might work best to fill a small bucket, or how to get sand through the narrow opening of a bottle. Opportunities to increase their understanding of math occur when children use one-to-one correspondence while filling each slot of an ice-cube tray with a pebble or count how many scoops it takes to fill a small tub with water. The following lists sensory materials typically found in preschool classrooms.

- Sensory bottles and tubs
- Wet and dry materials, such as water, dish soap, salt, sand, pebbles, shredded paper, water beads, and birdseed
- Tools and utensils, such as measuring spoons, funnels, cups, PVC pipe, and tongs
- Recycled items, such as plastic bottles, cardboard tubes, and food containers
- Natural materials, such as rocks, sticks, shells, and leaves
- Loose parts, such as cotton balls, pompoms, beads, marbles, and gems
- Toy vehicles and animals

MATERIALS IN ACTION—CONVERSATION

Several children are at the science shelf exploring the pet-food sensory bottles. Each bottle has a different type of pet food in it, from goldfish flakes to dog treats. A photograph of the corresponding pet is attached to the bottle. A lively conversation ensues in which the children tell each other what pets they have at home, what their names are, and what pets they wish they had.

Sensory Bottle

Materials

Plastic water or soda
    bottle with lid
Hot-glue gun
    (adult use only)
Water
Baby oil

Food coloring
Glitter
Sand
Small items, such as
    letter beads or shapes

4. Run a bead of hot glue around the lid before
screwing it back on.

1. Fill a bottle two-thirds full with water.

2. Add some baby oil.

3. Get creative: add food coloring, glitter,
waterproof confetti, letter beads, sand, or
other small items.

Scented Spice Jars

Materials

Empty plastic spice or herb containers
Cotton balls
Extracts, such as vanilla, lemon, or peppermint

1. Pull the plastic shaker lid off the container.

2. Place a few drops of an extract on a
cotton ball.

3. Place the cotton ball in the spice bottle.

4. Replace the plastic shaker lid.

5. Screw on the bottle lid to keep the scent fresh.

COLLECT DRY MATERIALS FOR USE IN SENSORY TABLES

While sand might be the most traditional dry material to put in a sensory table, many teachers find that children enjoy pouring and scooping almost anything they add. Switching it up creates interest and acts as an invitation for children to investigate. Think about the texture, color, and sounds made by a material. The following is a list of ideas of dry materials to add to the sensory table.

- Confetti
- Salt
- Coffee

- Pebbles
- Shredded paper
- Birdseed

- Green leaves
- Autumn leaves
- Dirt

- Mud
- Rocks
- Aquarium rocks

- Pea gravel
- Colored sand
- Fossils
- Driftwood

- Small sticks or twigs
- Wheat stalks
- Seashells
- Pinecones

- Grass
- Craft feathers
- Hay

- Gourds
- Acorns

COLLECT TOOLS AND UTENSILS FOR SENSORY TABLES

The next time you clean out your own kitchen cabinets or dig through the recycling bin, you will find a multitude of utensils that can be used in the sensory table. Provide a variety of sizes and shapes of bottles, scoops, and containers. Each different utensil will add to the children's creativity and exploration. The following lists ideas for tools and utensils for use in a sensory table.

For use with dry materials:

- Sifters
- Egg cartons
- Plastic spoons
- Colanders
- Combs
- Yogurt or fruit cups

- Spice containers
- PVC pipe and elbows
- Laundry scoops
- Laundry-soap lids
- Small pitchers
- Interlocking blocks

- Plastic bowls
- Ladles
- Wire whisks
- Gelatin molds
- Measuring cups
- Measuring spoons

- Funnels
- Kitchen gadgets
- Plastic food containers
- Plastic bottles
- Recycled food trays

MATERIALS IN ACTION—ATTENTION SPAN

Marisa goes over to the sensory table to find acorns and various utensils, including a large plastic jar. She begins filling the jar with the acorns by scooping and pouring them with her hands. When the jar is full to overflowing, she dumps the contents and begins again. She does this multiple times before moving to another activity.

- ▓ Butter tubs
- ▓ Ice-cube trays
- ▓ Muffin tins
- ▓ Gardening utensils
- ▓ Tongs
- ▓ Egg beaters
- ▓ Berry baskets
- ▓ Scoops

For use with wet materials:

- ▓ Pipettes
- ▓ Turkey basters
- ▓ Straws
- ▓ Cups
- ▓ Funnels
- ▓ Rubber fishing lures
- ▓ Craft-foam fish
- ▓ Aquarium nets
- ▓ Ping-Pong balls
- ▓ Water wheels
- ▓ Sponges
- ▓ Washcloths
- ▓ Clear flexible tubing
- ▓ Strainers
- ▓ Berry baskets

MATERIALS IN ACTION—BIG AND LITTLE

Sam and Rebecca are scooping and pouring the variety of beans that have been placed in the sensory table. Sam begins using a small scoop to fill a berry basket with beans. When it is full, he picks up the basket and watches the beans fall through the mesh. He shakes the basket a little to assist in the process. All of the smaller beans fall through, leaving only the larger lima beans. He tells Rebecca, "Look! The little ones fell out, but the big ones stayed!"

Using Water in the Sensory Table

Just water and a few scoops is enough to engage children at the sensory table, but you can add food coloring or bubble bath to spark their interest. As they give the baby dolls a bath or wash the dishes from the dramatic-play area, the children will be taking care of their classroom while they play. The following is a list of ideas of items to add to the water in the sensory table.

- Food coloring
- Scented extracts, such as peppermint
- Baby wash or child-friendly shampoo
- Ice cubes
- Colored ice cubes
- Ice cubes with small plastic figures frozen inside
- Large blocks of ice (freeze water in butter tubs)
- Ice balls (freeze water in water balloons)

- Baby dolls
- Play dishes
- Toy vehicles
- Frogs with craft-foam lily pads
- Penguins and Styrofoam icebergs
- Logs (thick sticks) and frogs

Two children are working together at the sensory table that has been partially filled with sudsy water. They are each using measuring cups to pour water through funnels and into plastic bottles. Deana's bottle falls over, causing a small amount of water to splash onto Tarek's shirt. He appears frustrated as he calls out to the teacher that Deana splashed him. The teacher comes over, and after a short discussion, everyone agrees that it was an accident. A few moments later, Tarek's bottle falls over and splashes Deana. After pointing out that she has been splashed, she reassures Tarek that it was just an accident. The play continues without incident.

CREATE UTENSILS AND MATERIALS FOR USE IN THE SENSORY TABLE

In addition to collecting utensils for the sensory table, you can create some, too. Young children enjoy and seem to have an internal drive to transport materials, so making structures with varying levels and holes for the sensory table opens up new learning possibilities.

Soda-Bottle Funnels

Materials

Plastic soda bottles in various sizes
Duct tape
Scissors

1. Cut the tops off varying sizes of plastic bottles.

2. Cover any sharp edges with duct tape.

3. Encourage the children to experiment with the funnels in the sensory table.

Sand Combs

Materials

Plastic lids, such as butter-tub lids
Scissors

1. Cut the lids in half using zigzag or wavy patterns.

2. Encourage the children to use the lids to create patterns in the sand.

Sieves and Colanders

Materials

Plastic containers, such as butter tubs

Nail (adult use only)

Hammer (adult use only)

1. Use a nail to punch holes in the bottoms of recycled food containers.

2. Encourage the children to use the colanders in the water table or the sand box.

COLLECT VEHICLES AND WILDLIFE TOYS FOR THE SENSORY TABLE

To promote dramatic play at the sensory table, you can add vehicles and animal toys. Search the supply closets at your center or make a quick trip to the dollar store for snakes, frogs, and insects, or visit the sporting goods store for fishing lures. The following lists some ideas for items to add to the sensory table.

- Cars
- Trucks
- Boats
- Tractors
- Construction vehicles
- Farm animals
- Wild animals
- Dinosaurs
- Whales
- Insects
- Rubber snakes
- Frogs

- Lizards
- Rubber ducks
- Counting bears

Elijah is enjoying playing at the sensory table by himself. The table is full of sand and various utensils such as plastic containers, measuring cups and spoons, funnels, and cups. He has chosen to use a tablespoon to fill a large, clear plastic container. He works slowly but methodically. Inch by inch, the bottle gets filled. Occasionally, he is distracted by something else happening in the room, but then he gets right back to it. When the container is full, he says, "Look, Ms. Vanessa! I filled it all up!"

CREATE COMBINATIONS FOR THE SENSORY TABLE

You might choose to provide just a few items in the sensory table to see how children use them, or you could keep adding materials to spice things up. Whether you decide to add common items or throw in something unusual, the key is to see what engages the children and sparks their interest. The following lists some combinations of items you could try.

- Rocks and water
- Red objects and utensils with red sand
- Shaving cream and spoons
- Pompoms or cotton balls and tongs
- Styrofoam and craft sticks
- Plastic flowers and pots in dirt
- Craft jewels in sand
- Gold nuggets in pea gravel (use gold spray paint)
- Plastic frogs and craft-foam lily pads
- Golf balls and ice-cream scoops
- Magnetic marbles or wands
- Metallic and nonmetallic objects with magnetic wands
- Aquarium plants and pea gravel in water
- Slippery cords from old window blinds, and red pompoms

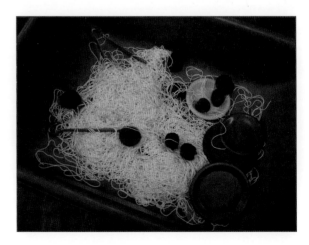

10 Books and Print Materials

The preschoolers enjoyed the grocery-store props that their teachers had added to the dramatic-play area of their classroom. As the week went on, the teachers continued to add props they felt the children might be interested in. Mr. Thomas brought flyers from the local grocery store and placed them on the table near the center. Several children were immediately interested because they recognized the store logo. They each had stories to tell about trips to the grocery store and what their families had bought. Samar opened the flyer and began pointing out foods that he liked. Other children joined in. Lucy pointed out that there were numbers next to the pictures. Samar explained to her that the numbers told you how much the food cost. The conversation turned to talking about how much money was needed to buy the food they wanted.

Daily reading is one of the most important contributions adults can make to young children's learning and development. Reading enhances children's listening-comprehension skills, builds their vocabulary, and increases their understanding of concepts. Just hearing the sounds of language aids children in their speech production. The content of books can promote the development of empathy and can assist in children's growing ability to see the perspectives of others. When children are caught up in a good story, they can focus for longer periods of time, which helps increase their attention spans. In addition to reading with children, providing a wide variety of book and print materials for self-directed exploration will allow children the opportunity to learn about the purposes and concepts of print.

INVITING CHILDREN TO EXPLORE BOOK AND PRINT MATERIALS

Make the book area of your classroom cozy and inviting by adding rugs, couches, pillows, blankets, and stuffed animals, so that children will be eager to curl up and explore a good book. Artfully arranging books on a bookshelf or in buckets are great ways to display books, but also think about placing books strategically throughout the classroom. Books about architecture or construction vehicles can be placed in the block area. A book about shapes can be placed in the manipulative area. Nonfiction books about nature and animals can be placed on the science shelf. Children particularly enjoy classroom books made by the teachers or those that they have made themselves. They also enjoy other forms of print in addition to books; magazines and catalogs will often catch children's attention.

CREATING SPECIAL SPACES FOR EXPLORING BOOKS

Entice children into the book area by creating cozy nooks where they can snuggle up with a favorite story.

Reading House

Materials

Large cardboard box
Colored tape
Scissors
Blanket
Pillows

1. Turn the box on its side, and cut a large opening—big enough for a child to climb in and out of easily.

2. Tape around the edges of the opening.

3. Open the flaps on the top of the box.

4. Pull up two of them and cut off the corners to create a triangular shape. This will represent a roof.

5. Tape the edges with colored tape.

6. Inside the reading house, place a blanket or pillow.

Card-Table Cave

Materials

Card table

Blanket, sheet, or scrap fabric

Pillows

1. Set up a card table in the book area.

2. Cover the table with fabric. Let the fabric drape down the sides of the table.

3. Place pillows under the table, if you wish.

BOOK AND PRINT MATERIALS SUPPORT LEARNING ACROSS THE DOMAINS

In addition to the obvious language and literacy benefits that books and print materials provide, they also enhance children's development across the domains. As children explore books, they are building on their print concepts. As they "read" books they have memorized, they might play with sounds in language such as alliteration and rhyme. They might retell favorite stories, which will increase their comprehension abilities.

Engagement with books adds to their fine and gross motor development. When holding books and turning the pages, they are afforded opportunities to develop their fine motor skills. Gross motor skills are enhanced when they act out stories and books. Sharing books with friends and telling each other stories provides opportunities for children to connect with each other and further develop their social skills. They might

MATERIALS IN ACTION—PRINT CONCEPTS

A classroom interest in pets leads a teacher to add some dog and cat magazines to the bookshelf. After snack, Josie chooses a magazine and sits down on a beanbag to look at it. As she turns the pages, the teacher notices her talking to herself about the pictures. The teacher also notices that Josie is careful when she turns the pages so that she does not miss any. She began at the beginning of the magazine and made it almost to the end; then, she put the magazine back on the shelf and went to play with her friends.

Jan is sitting in the laundry basket that has been placed near the bookshelf. She has maneuvered a pillow to rest her back against, and her knees are bent so that she fits inside. Her arms are wrapped around a stuffed bear, and she is holding a book so that they can both see the pages. As she looks at each page, she tells the bear what is happening in the pictures. She changes the tone and pitch of her voice to match the actions she describes. When she gets to the last page, she says, "The end!"

also explore emotions and empathy when connecting with the themes of a book and a story's characters.

Cognitive development is enhanced as children build on concepts found in the content of books and stories. Nonfiction books and print materials provide opportunities to explore a multitude of concepts. Children might also compare books in terms of size, illustration, or topics.

BOOKS AND PRINT MATERIALS TYPICALLY FOUND IN PRESCHOOL CLASSROOMS

Many preschool classrooms have a designated area or center for books and storytelling. If any of the children in your classroom speak a language other than English at home, be sure to include materials in those languages as well as English. The following lists materials typically included there.

- Fiction stories
- Nonfiction informational texts
- Magazines
- Posters
- Puppets and story props
- Encyclopedias
- Newspapers
- Catalogs
- Maps
- Store flyers
- Leaflets
- Brochures
- Menus

CREATE BOOKS

You can stock your book area with commercially produced books, but it's also fun to create your own. You can make books about field trips your class has taken; class activities, such as "How We Made Pancakes"; friends; and so on. Use photos of the children to encourage their excitement and interest.

Consider the children's interests, and make reading materials that will enhance their understandings. These books could be about animals, dinosaurs, children from other cultures, shapes, types of homes, weather, flowers—the possibilities are endless!

Page-Protector Book

Materials
Copy paper
Plastic page protectors
Images of your choice
Glue stick
Scissors
Marker
Yarn, ribbon, or metal key rings

1. Choose images that reflect a topic the children are interested in.

2. Cut out and glue the images to the paper.

3. Near the image on the page, write a word or two that describes the image. For example, underneath an image of a frog, you could write *green frog*.

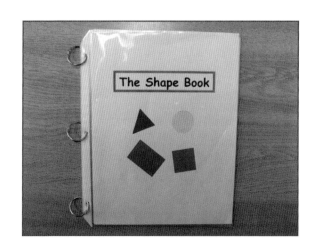

4. When you've made the pages, slide them into page protectors.

5. Hold the pages together with yarn or ribbon tied through the holes in the page protectors. Alternatively, you could use metal key rings.

Baggie Book

Materials

6 pint-size resealable freezer bags	Scissors
Card stock	Glue
Stapler	Images of your choice
Duct tape	Markers

1. Cut six pieces of card stock to the size that will easily fit into the plastic bags.
2. Create the book content on pieces of card stock using the fronts and backs.
3. Slide the pages into baggies.
4. Stack them together in the correct order, and seal the baggies.
5. Staple all six bags together at the top edge above the seals.
6. Cover the staples with duct tape to create a binding.

Binder Book

Materials

Half-inch binder	Images for book content
Page protectors	Scissors
Card stock	Glue

1. Create the book content on the fronts and backs of card stock.
2. Slide the pages into page protectors.
3. Place the pages into the binder.

Variation: Instead of using page protectors, you can laminate the card stock and punch holes in the pages.

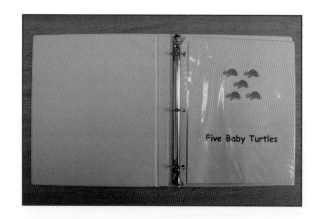

Accordion Book

Materials

Card stock

Images for book content

Glue

Scissors

Clear packing tape

1. Cut the card stock into squares in the quantity and size needed for your content.
2. Create the book pages.
3. Laminate the pages.

4. Place the first two pages side by side. Use one piece of packing tape to join the two pages together.

5. Place the third page next to the second page, and repeat the process.

6. Continue until all pages are connected in one strip.

7. Fold the book accordion style.

Mini Photo-Album Books

Materials
Mini photo albums
Images for book content
White paper

1. Cut the paper to the correct size to slide into the album.

2. Create the book content on the paper pages.

3. Slide the completed pages into the album.

4. Cut out any unused pages from the photo album if not all pages are used.

MATERIALS IN ACTION—FRIENDS

Earlier in the week, Miss Natasha suggested making a class book of the children's artwork. Anyone who was interested could draw a picture to be added to the book. Miss Natasha then added a photo of each child on the opposing page from that child's artwork, so that when they turned pages, they would see who created each piece. She placed the book on the classroom bookshelf. For the rest of the week, the children spent time looking at the book and showing each other the photos and art. On Friday, a child who was not interested in participating earlier in the week made a drawing and asked Miss Natasha if it could be put in the class book. Another child commented, "Now that's everybody! That's all our friends!"

CREATE SONG AND STORY PROPS

Props for songs and stories allow for active participation. Children can hold and manipulate the pieces as they tell a new story or retell a favorite. The props help children remember the sequence of a story, which contributes to comprehension.

Sequence Sticks

Materials

Recycled paint stir stick	Card stock
Adhesive Velcro tape	Scissors
Story or song images	Glue

1. Cut 1-inch squares from card stock, and cut out the images to illustrate the song or story.

2. Glue the song or story images to the squares.

3. Laminate or cover the cards with clear tape for durability.

4. Attach a strip of the hook side of the Velcro to the entire length of the stir stick.

5. Cut the loop side of the Velcro strip into squares.

6. Attach the Velcro squares to the backside of the images.

7. Attach the images to the stir stick.

8. Children can remove and replace images as they sing the song or tell the story.

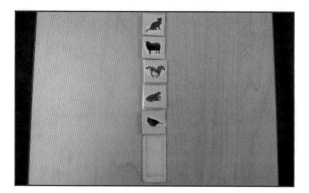

Song or Story Cube

Materials

Cardboard box	Glue
Butcher paper	Scissors
Song or story images	Marker
Clear packing tape	

1. Wrap the box with butcher paper, and secure the paper with glue.

2. Add song or story images to the sides of the box.

3. Completely cover the cube with clear tape for added durability.

4. Children can sing a song or tell a story as they turn and flip the box to see the images.

Pocket-Chart Song or Story Sequence Strips

Materials

Pocket chart	Images
Sentence strips	Marker
Scissors	Glue

1. Cut the sentence strips into lengths that fit your pocket chart.

2. Write a line from a song or story on each of the strips.

3. Add images to support understanding and illustrate the song or story.

4. Laminate the strips or cover them with clear packing tape for durability.

5. Children can place the strips in the chart as they sing the song or tell the story.

Character Headbands

Materials

Sentence strip	Marker
Story or song characters	Glue
Adhesive Velcro tape	Clear packing tape
Scissors	

1. Cut a sentence strip into a length that will fit around a preschooler's head, plus an additional 4 inches.

2. Glue a character image on the center of each strip, and label if desired.

3. Laminate or cover the headband with clear packing tape for added durability.

4. Attach Velcro tape to the ends so that the headband is adjustable and easy to put on and remove.

5. The children can wear the headbands and pretend to be characters when they sing songs or tell stories.

Five Speckled Frogs

Materials

Cardboard tube   Clear packing tape

Brown and blue   Marker

   construction paper   Scissors

5 frog images   Glue

1. Cut the brown construction paper into 2" x 8" strips. Make five strips.

2. Fold the strips in half with the open ends at the top, and glue a frog image to the top half of each of the folded brown flaps.

3. Write a numeral from 1 to 5 on each flap under the frog image.

4. Cut five sections of blue construction paper into 2" x 1" strips. Cut one edge of each in a wavy pattern.

5. Turn the brown flaps over with the open ends at the bottom, and glue a blue piece to the back of each brown flap.

6. Open the flaps, and lay them flat. Cover each strip with clear packing tape for durability.

7. Wrap the strip around the tube, but leave a little room so that it will rotate around the tube easily.

8. Glue or tape the extra length on the ends together.

9. Continue until all five flaps are lined up on the cardboard tube.

10. Children can flip the frogs down as they sing the song.

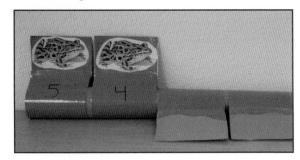

Five Little Monkeys

Materials

Recycled tissue box   Glue

Blue and white   Clear packing tape

   construction paper   Hot-glue gun

5 craft sticks   (adult use only)

5 monkey images   Utility knife

Scissors   (adult use only)

1. Draw or print out five monkey pictures.

2. Cut out the monkeys, and cover the images with clear packing tape or laminate them for durability.

3. Attach each monkey to a craft stick with hot glue.

4. Wrap and decorate the tissue box to resemble a bed: wrap part of it with white construction paper, then cover the rest with the blue construction paper.

5. Completely cover the wrapped box with clear tape for added durability.

6. Cut five slits in the top of the box with the utility knife.

7. Slide a monkey stick in each slit.

8. Children can remove and replace monkeys as they sing the song.

11 Felt and Magnet Boards

The children immediately noticed the magnetic board when they walked into the classroom on Monday morning. Their teacher had added a sun that had rays labeled with the numerals from 1 to 20. Dora and Jacklyn took turns taking the sun and rays apart and putting them back together

again. Dora noticed something interesting about the rays once the sun was put together. She said, "This one is yellow. This one is orange. This one is yellow. It makes a pattern!" Jacklyn added, "One is orange. Two is yellow. Three is orange. Four is—it does make a pattern!"

In our ever-changing technological world, some may think that traditional felt boards are old-fashioned, but early childhood teachers know better. Felt-board activities provide true hands-on learning opportunities across all of the developmental domains, from the language used for storytelling to the fine motor skill involved in getting the pieces arranged just right. Felt boards are also one of the least expensive ways that teachers can enhance the classroom.

Magnet boards share many of the same benefits as felt boards and create novel experiences for children. Both types of boards allow children to remember the sequence of a story or song because they are prompted by the pieces in front of them. Children can use their own creativity to invent a story or song from the pieces available. In addition to storytelling, these boards can also provide opportunities for counting, sorting, matching, and sequencing. When children work together at the boards, they get all the social benefits of negotiating for favorite pieces, sharing, and taking turns. Whether children work alone or with others, felt and magnet boards create learning experiences that stick!

INVITING CHILDREN TO EXPLORE FELT AND MAGNET BOARDS

Boards of either type allow teachers countless possibilities. Smaller boards can be used by individual children, and larger boards work well for small groups. When pieces go missing, it is easy to make replacement pieces. When there seem not to be enough pieces to go around, grab some felt and quickly make more. Create felt pieces that relate to children's interests or curriculum concepts, or attach adhesive felt or magnetic tape to the back of laminated paper pieces. Few materials are so versatile.

FELT AND MAGNET ACTIVITIES SUPPORT LEARNING ACROSS THE DOMAINS

Felt and magnet boards offer many opportunities for children to enhance their skills. As the children engage with the materials, they can develop language and literacy skills, fine motor skills, social-emotional skills, science and math learning, and cognitive skills.

Felt and magnet activities can enhance language and literacy skills when children tell stories or sing songs that correlate to the pieces being used. They might have conversations about the materials, utilizing their related background knowledge. Through storytelling with pieces, children can remember the parts of a story, which aids in their comprehension. Trying to place the pieces of a story or activity can be tricky and provides lots of practice for children's fine motor development. They have to coordinate their physical skills to get the pieces to stay where they want them. When working on larger boards with larger pieces, children have opportunities to build on gross motor skills.

Engaging with felt and flannel boards can be a social activity that enhances the skills of working with others, taking turns, and sharing. Children have opportunities to express feelings while telling stories or singing songs. Self-regulatory skills are promoted through patience and perseverance.

Felt and magnet board activities can support cognitive skills as well. Children can build on their concept of spatial awareness through placement and sequencing of pieces. They may have to solve problems related to how to create a desired pattern or how to place the pieces for a story. They might compare and contrast the different sizes and shapes of the pieces they are working with.

FELT AND MAGNETIC MATERIALS TYPICALLY FOUND IN PRESCHOOL CLASSROOMS

Many preschool classrooms have a designated area or center for felt and magnet boards. The following lists materials typically included.

- Variety of types and sizes of felt boards
- Magnet boards made of cookies sheets, file cabinets, and stove-burner covers
- Activity sets for boards, such as matching or storytelling
- Purchased or created board pieces

CREATE FLANNEL BOARDS AND PIECES

Felt boards are simple and easy to make. Follow these directions to make a basic board—then get creative!

Basic Flannel Board

Materials

Cardboard or foam board	Scissors
Utility knife	Hot-glue gun (adult use only)
(adult use only)	Duct tape
Flannel	Picture frame (optional)

1. Cut a piece of cardboard or foam board to the desired size. I you want to create a finished look, cut the board to fit inside a picture frame.

2. Cut a piece of flannel two inches longer and wider than your board. **Tip:** Use flannel instead of felt. It is less expensive and more durable, and felt pieces easily stick to it.

3. Lay the flannel front-side down on a table. Center the board on top.

4. Run a bead of hot glue down one side of the board, next to the edge. Fold the flannel over the edge of the board, and smooth the fabric.

5. Repeat on the opposite side so that you can pull the flannel taut to reduce wrinkling.

6. Repeat on the other two sides to cover the board.

7. When the glue is cool, cover the rough edges of fabric with duct tape.

8. If you are using a picture frame, fit the flannel board inside it, and secure the board with duct tape.

Laminated Activity Pieces

Materials

Photographs

Magazines

Drawings

Clear contact paper or
clear packing tape

Adhesive Velcro tape

Scissors

1. Cut out images you want to use. These could fit with a theme, such as animals that live in a jungle or different kinds of homes. They could represent characters in a story. You could also make color copies of drawings and cut them out.

2. Laminate or cover the images with clear tape or contact paper.

3. Cut squares of Velcro tape, and stick one on the back of each image.

4. Encourage the children to use the images on the flannel board.

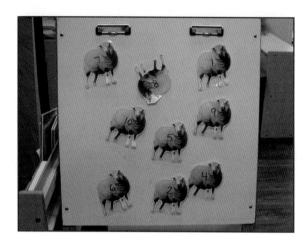

MATERIALS IN ACTION—COMPARISON OF SIZE

Several felt rainbow sets have been placed at the flannel board. Each set consists of six concentric half circles in different colors. When stacked on top of each other from largest to smallest, the pieces create a rainbow. Bethany disassembles the rainbows and spreads the pieces across the board. After some time spent in exploration, she begins matching colors to create complete circles. Each color makes a circle of a different size. A friend joins her, and Bethany suggests that they put the big red ones next to the little purple ones.

CREATE MAGNETIC BOARDS AND PIECES

Many preschool classrooms already have magnetic boards in the form of wall-mounted dry-erase boards or the flipside of an easel. If not, you can easily create them using cookie sheets, pizza pans, stove-burner covers, decorative tins and lids, or the side of a filing cabinet.

Magnetic Activity Pieces

Materials

Photographs

Magazines

Drawings

Clear contact paper or clear packing tape

Magnetic adhesive tape

Scissors

1. Cut out images you want to use. These could fit with a theme, such as animals that live in the ocean. They could be flowers with numerals written on them. You could also make color copies of drawings and cut them out.

2. Laminate or cover the images with clear tape or contact paper.

3. Cut pieces of magnetic tape, and stick one on the back of each image.

4. Encourage the children to use the images on the magnetic board.

CREATE ACTIVITY SETS FOR FLANNEL OR MAGNETIC BOARDS

You can create sets that connect to the children's interests, curriculum concepts, and developing skills. For example, use Magnetic Classroom Friends at the beginning of a new school year to help children learn the names of their new classmates.

Magnetic Classroom Friends

Materials

Digital camera
Clear packing tape
Adhesive magnetic tape
Scissors

1. Take full-body photographs of the children in your classroom.

2. Print and cut out the images.

3. Laminate or cover the images with clear packing tape for added durability.

4. Cut pieces of magnetic tape and attach one to the back of each image.

5. Flannel-board variation: Cut sticky-back felt pieces to fit the images, and attach these instead of magnetic tape to each photo.

Flannel-Board Pizza

Materials

Pizza image
Clear packing tape
Scissors
Sticky-back felt

1. Cut the pizza image into equal pieces. **Tip:** To get equally sized pieces, fold the pizza in half and cut on the fold. Repeat until you have eight pieces.

2. Laminate or cover the pieces with clear packing tape for added durability.

3. Attach sticky-back felt to backs of the pieces.

4. Magnetic-board variation: Attach magnetic tape instead of sticky-back felt to the backs of the pieces.

Adrian enjoyed using the jack-o'-lantern felt pieces that he found in a basket next to the flannel board in his classroom. There were six pumpkins, and he lined them up in a row across the board. He then began to carefully place the facial features on each one, making sure each had two eyes, a nose, and a mouth. His teacher observed that he consistently found matching shapes for the eyes. In one instance, he could not find a matching small triangle similar to the one he had already placed on a pumpkin, so he removed it and found two matching squares to use instead.

Felt Castle

Materials

Felt in a variety of colors
Scissors

1. Cut out castle parts from the felt: main building, towers, roofs of towers, flags, door, and windows.

2. Encourage the children to build castles on the flannel board.

Felt Dress-Up People

Materials

Felt in a variety of colors and patterns
Scissors
Permanent marker

1. Cut out people shapes.

2. Cut out a variety of clothing: shirts, pants, dresses, ties, hats, and so on.

3. Cut out hair and moustaches.

4. Draw little faces on the felt people.

5. Encourage the children to mix and match the clothing and features of the dress-up people on the flannel board.

Seasonal Sets
Materials
Felt in a variety of colors
Scissors

1. Decide on the image you want to create. For example, for winter, you could create a felt snowman. For summer, a felt bucket with items such as shells, a shovel, and toys to place in it. Or, you could create a felt beach with water, shells, crabs, and birds. For spring, felt flower pieces, including stems, flowers, leaves, and butterflies. For autumn, a felt tree and leaves.

2. Cut out the shapes and encourage the children to explore them at the flannel board.

MATERIALS IN ACTION—POSITION IN SPACE

Several children are at the flannel board playing with the "Five Little Monkeys Jumping on the Bed" felt pieces. They are singing the song while making the monkeys jump and also jumping themselves. One child is making the monkeys fall off the bed by throwing them in the air. Each time he does it, the others laugh and scramble to pick the monkey back up and place it above the bed so he can do it again. Sometimes a monkey lands on top of another monkey. Children laugh and the game turns to stacking the monkeys one on top of the other.

Thrifty Teacher's Guide to Creative Learning Centers

Holiday Sets

Materials

Felt in a variety of colors
Scissors

1. Decide on the holiday you wish to represent. You could make a felt menorah for Hanukkah, a felt tree and decorations for Christmas, a felt flag for the Fourth of July, or felt pumpkins and faces for Halloween. Consider the cultures of the children in your classroom, and make sets to honor them.

2. Cut out the shapes and place them near the flannel board.

3. Encourage the children to explore the sets, and talk with them about what they represent.

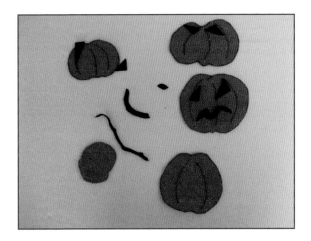

CREATE SONG AND STORY BOARDS

Felt pieces are great tools to support children's understanding of story sequence and characters. Make felt characters and scenes to go along with the children's favorite stories or books you are exploring together. You can also make felt pieces to go with favorite songs.

 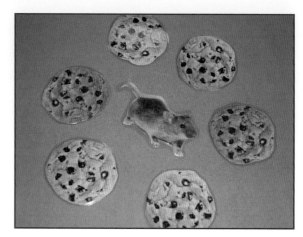

The Three Little Pigs

Materials

Felt in gray, pink, yellow, brown, and red
Scissors
Permanent markers

1. Cut out the three pigs' houses: yellow for straw, brown for sticks, and red for brick.

2. Use the markers to draw in details on the houses.

3. Create a pile of straw from the yellow felt and a pile of sticks from the brown felt. These will represent the houses that the wolf blows down.

4. Cut out a wolf face from the gray felt.

5. Cut out three pig faces from the pink felt.

6. Encourage the children to retell the story using the felt pieces.

12 Puppets

The prekindergarten teachers held a Puppet Show Week for the children. They added several different types of stages, a great variety of puppets, and other show props such as popcorn buckets and tickets. Throughout the week, the children took turns producing, creating, directing, and acting in their own shows in addition to pretending to be audience members who bought tickets and ate popcorn. The teachers noticed that the children took being an audience member very seriously and would sit quietly to watch the shows. The children also enjoyed making their own puppets. Their teachers were quick to add more resources to the art area. This led to the children building their own puppet stages, and the hunt for boxes began.

Children enjoy puppets and creating their own puppet shows. Fortunately, puppets are easy and inexpensive to make. From finger puppets to marionettes, children delight in moving puppets about and making them talk. This not only works to further their language development, but it also aids in their ability to see the perspective of others. Whichever role they choose, from director to actor to audience member, there are opportunities for creativity, self-regulation, and attention. Let the shows begin!

INVITING CHILDREN TO ENGAGE WITH PUPPETS

Enhance the classroom environment by setting up a specific area with puppets and a stage or by providing a variety of puppets throughout the classroom. Puppets placed in the book area invite children to use them to retell or act out a story. You can also connect puppets to curriculum interests or themes. For example, a classroom interest in insects might lead to finding or creating insect puppets. Finger puppets and marionettes will also entice the children to engage in puppet play.

PUPPET PLAY SUPPORTS LEARNING ACROSS THE DOMAINS

Puppet play can support learning in and across the domains of language and literacy development; fine and gross motor development; socio-emotional development; and science, math, and cognitive development.

Puppets can promote children's language and literacy development when children talk like a puppet character and have conversations with each other during puppet play. As they use puppets to tell and retell stories, they might use new vocabulary and syntax. The puppets can also assist in their growing ability to recall the sequence of a story through the actions of the characters. Finger and stick puppets provide opportunities for children to develop their fine motor skills. They have to figure out how to coordinate their actions when using a puppet stage so that the audience can see the action. Gross motor skills are exercised when children work to make a marionette walk across the floor or stage.

MATERIALS IN ACTION—PERSONAL BOUNDARIES

Marcus has found the alligator felt puppet and is going around the room finding children to "eat." As he moves the puppet close to Sophia's face, she emphatically states, "I don't like that. Stop, Marcus!" He tries again, and she yells, "No!" while moving away. He turns toward Michael, who laughs and does not seem to mind the alligator chomping on his arm. Marcus continues on with varying success. Some children enjoy the game; others do not. When he comes back to Sophia again, she gets angry and calls out to the teacher. Miss Janie comes over to see what is happening. After a brief discussion in which all parties agree that if someone does not like playing that way, then the other person should stop and find someone else to play with, Marcus moves on and does not come back to try Sophia again.

Puppet play supports children's social-emotional development as they cooperate to develop a puppet story or show. They can use the puppets to express emotions and also to recognize the emotion of a puppet someone else is using. When children participate as part of the audience and when they work through frustrations in getting the puppets to do what they desire, they build their self-regulation skills.

Cognitive development is supported as children build on the concepts related to the stories and actions of their puppets. Opportunities for problem solving happen when children are trying to figure out how to get their puppets to move. Positioning of puppets when doing a show develops children's understanding of spatial awareness and the perspective of others. The following lists puppet materials typically found in preschool classrooms.

- Puppets made from mittens, gloves, sticks, paper bags, socks, or spoons

- Marionettes
- Puppet stages created from boxes or doorways

Mitten Puppets

Materials

Felt in a variety of colors   Hot-glue gun
Scissors   (adult use only)

1. Fold a standard-size sheet of felt in half.
2. Cut the top to the desired shape.

3. Open the felt, and attach features to the half that will be the puppet's face.
4. Squeeze hot glue across the top and open side before folding the felt over to create a mitten. Leave the bottom unglued.

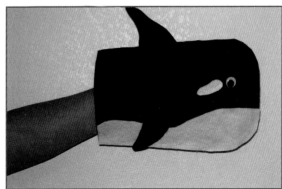

Glove Puppets

Materials

Recycled gardening glove
Craft foam
Adhesive Velcro tape
Hot-glue gun (adult use only)
Permanent markers

1. Create song or story characters using craft foam and markers.

2. Attach small squares of the hook side of the Velcro to the character pieces.

3. Attach small squares of the loop side of the Velcro to the end of each finger using hot glue. **Tip:** Be consistent when applying the Velcro tape so that the loop side is on the fingers and the hook is on the pieces (or vice versa).

4. You can also attach a small strip of the loop side to the palm area and on the back to create storage places for the pieces as you tell the story or sing the song.

Dalia has a zebra sock puppet on her arm, and Tyler has a tiger sock puppet on his. They use their puppets to talk to each other on opposite sides of the puppet stage. The teacher overhears the following snippets of their conversation:

DALIA: Tiger, what are you doing?

TYLER: I'm going to the movie.

DALIA: I want to go! Can I go with you, Tiger?

TYLER: Yes, you can.

DALIA: Let's hurry! Hurry, Tiger!

TYLER: Okay, okay! Run! (They make their puppets run back and forth across the stage.)

Knit Glove Puppets

Materials

Recycled knit gloves
Song or story character images
Adhesive Velcro tape
Clear packing tape
Scissors

1. Cut out song or story character images.

2. Cover each with clear tape or laminate them for added durability.

3. Cut squares of Velcro tape.

4. Attach the hook side of the tape to character, and save the loop side for another project. The characters will now stick to the knit gloves.

5. Encourage the children to sing or retell stories using the gloves.

Sock Puppets

Materials

Socks	Cardboard or card stock
Felt	Scissors
Googly eyes	Glue
Buttons	Needle and thread
Fabric paint	(adult use only)
Chenille stems	

1. Find socks at a dollar store.

2. Decorate each sock with felt, googly eyes, buttons, paint, or chenille stems. The character possibilities are endless!

3. To create a mouth, fold a piece of cardboard or card stock in half. Glue on a piece of felt.

4. Put your hand into the sock puppet, and glue the mouth into the sock where your hand opens and closes.

Finger Puppets

Materials

Felt in a variety of colors	Hot-glue gun
Googly eyes	(adult use only)
Black permanent markers	Scissors

1. Cut two pieces of felt slightly larger than your finger. Make sure that, when they are glued together, they will fit over your finger with room to spare.

2. Glue the fronts and backs together, leaving an opening at the bottom.

3. When the glue is dry, turn the finger puppets inside out.

4. Decorate as you wish.

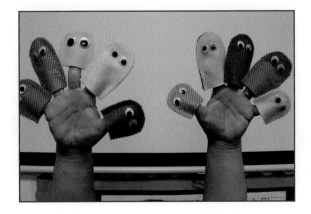

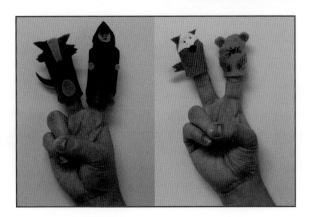

Stick Puppets

Materials

Craft foam

Paper

Card stock or cardboard

Chenille stems

Googly eyes

Craft sticks

Hot-glue gun (adult use only)

Photographs and other printed images

Clear contact paper

Scissors

1. Print or draw an image, then cut it out.

2. Laminate or cover it with clear contact paper for added durability.

3. Glue the image onto the end of a craft stick.

Variation: Cut out and decorate an image made of craft foam. Glue it onto the end of a craft stick.

Variation: For use with a Shoe Box Stick-Puppet Stage (page 186), glue the image onto the bottom of the craft stick, so that the children can manipulate the puppet from the stick at the top.

MATERIALS IN ACTION—STORY STRUCTURE

Marisa is sitting by herself on the beanbag chair in the book corner. She has three bear finger puppets on her fingers. One has a tie and represents the daddy bear. Another has a bow on her head to represent the mama bear. The smallest one is the baby bear. She begins telling the story of the three bears quietly to herself. For each part of the story, she focuses on the daddy bear first, then the mama, and finally the baby. She repeats this order for the chairs, the porridge, and the beds. As she talks, she alters her voice and mannerisms to mimic each character.

Cardboard Tube Puppets

Materials

Craft foam

Paper

Card stock or cardboard

Cardboard tube

Chenille stems

Googly eyes

Hot-glue gun (adult use only)

Photographs and other printed images

Clear contact paper

Scissors

1. Cardboard tubes can support larger images. Print or draw an image, then cut it out.

2. Laminate or cover it with clear contact paper for added durability.

3. Glue the image onto the end of a cardboard tube.

Variation: Cut out and decorate an image made of craft foam. Glue it onto the end of a cardboard tube.

MATERIALS IN ACTION—SINGING

Frankie found the animal stick puppets first thing on Monday morning. The set included farm animals and farmers of both genders. She sang quietly to herself as she manipulated the puppets: "Old MacDonald had a farm, e, i, e, i, o. And on his farm he had a . . ." As she sang an animal name, she would pick up that stick puppet and move it up and down. Then, she would make the animal sound at the appropriate time in the song. When she got through all the animals available, she started over before calling a friend over to join her.

Spoon Puppets

Materials

Spoons made of wood or plastic

Yarn

Fabric scraps

Googly eyes

Craft feathers

Felt

Scissors

Hot-glue gun (adult use only)

1. Turn the spoon over so that the back side is facing up.

2. Glue on hair, a hat, googly eyes, and other features and decorations.

3. Glue clothing onto the handle, leaving some room at the end so the children can easily hold the puppet.

4. To create arms and legs, attach craft sticks with hot glue or tie on chenille stems.

Elephant Marionette

Materials

Recycled oatmeal canister

Paper-towel tubes

Plastic twine or string

Cardboard scraps

2 jumbo craft sticks

Scissors

Hot-glue gun (adult use only)

Colored paper

Tape

Permanent marker

1. Cover or decorate the oatmeal canister for the elephant body.

2. Pierce two small holes on the top of the canister and four small holes on the bottom to allow for the strings that attach the legs.

3. Create the animal's head or print an image.

4. Glue cardboard on the head for added durability. Trim any excess from around the image.

5. Attach the animal's head to the bottom (closed end) of the canister with hot glue.

6. Cut eight 2-inch sections of cardboard tube, and decorate these to create legs.

7. Cut four elephant feet out of cardboard, ensuring that they are wider than the circumference of the tubes.

8. Pierce a small hole in the center of each foot.

9. Cut four pieces of string long enough to allow for each to run through the length of the animal and up to the handles.

10. Run each string through the holes in the canister, the cardboard tube legs, and the hole in the bottom of each foot. Tie knots underneath the feet and secure with tape.

11. Create the handle by making a *T* shape with the craft sticks, and secure them with hot glue.

12. Tie the top of each string to the handle.

Dancing Bird Marionette

Materials

2 large pompoms

2 small pompoms

Plastic bead necklace

Craft feathers

Googly eyes

Fishing line

2 jumbo craft sticks

Scissors

Hot-glue gun (adult use only)

1. Cut the bead necklace into one 4-inch section and two 2-inch sections.

2. Create the bird's body by attaching the 4-inch necklace piece to a large pompom with hot glue.

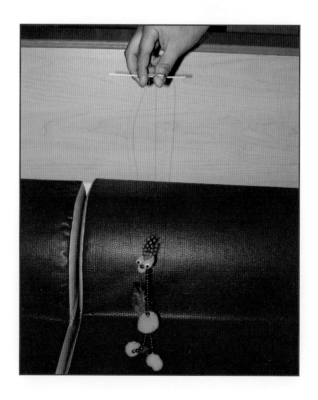

3. Glue the other large pompom on the other end of the 4-inch necklace to create a head.

4. Decorate the body and face as desired using googly eyes and feathers.

5. Glue the 2-inch sections of necklace to the bottom of the body to create legs.

6. Glue a small pompom on the bottom of each leg to create feet.

7. Cut four long pieces of fishing line. Tie one piece each to the head, body, and both feet.

8. Create the handle by making a *T* shape with the craft sticks, and secure them with hot glue.

9. Tie the top of each piece of fishing line to the handle.

Stuffed Animal Marionette

Materials
Stuffed animal with long arms and legs
2 jumbo craft sticks
Fishing line
Hot-glue gun (adult use only)

1. Cut five long pieces of fishing line.

2. Tie the pieces to the head, both hands, and both feet of the stuffed animal.

3. Create the handle by making a *T* shape with the craft sticks, and secure them with hot glue.

4. Tie the top of each piece of fishing line to the handle.

Sahar waves a princess spoon puppet in the air, saying, "I am the princess. A magical princess! And I will give you a wish." Jessie, who is playing nearby, jumps up and says she wants a wish. "Okay, you can have one wish. Just one. What do you want?" Sahar asks. Jessie thinks for a moment and then says, "I want to be the princess!" Sahar tells her no and reiterates that she is the magical princess. Jessie argues that Sahar has to give her the wish because that is what a magical princess does. When Sahar will not relent, Jessie loses interest and moves on to play with someone else. Sahar eventually finds several children who play along, and she grants them their imaginary wishes of "all the candy in the world" and "ice cream for dinner."

CREATE PUPPET STAGES

You and the children can make puppet stages from cardboard boxes or by simply turning a table on its side. Children can also perform puppet shows standing behind a cleared shelf.

Shoebox Stick-Puppet Stage

Materials

Recycled shoebox
Construction paper
Tissue paper
Glue
Utility knife (adult use only)
Scissors

1. Place the box on its side, and decorate the inside to create a scene of your choosing.

2. Use stick puppets made so that the character head and body are right-side up at the bottom of the craft stick. (See Stick Puppet instructions on page 181.)

Puppet Stage

Materials

Cardboard box
Utility knife (adult use only)
Paint

1. Cut a large rectangle in the front of the box. Cut another large rectangle in the back of the box that is a little lower than the one in the front.

2. You and the children can decorate the stage as desired.

3. Children can place the hand with the puppet through the hole in the back so that it can be seen through the hole in the front.

Curtained Puppet Stage

Materials

Cardboard box
Decorative paper
Pompoms
Yarn
Felt or fabric scraps
Utility knife (adult use only)
Hot-glue gun (adult use only)

1. Cut a large rectangle in the front of the box.

2. Cut another large rectangle in the back of the box that is a little lower than the one in the front. Children can place the hand with the puppet through the hole in the back so that it can be seen through the hole in the front.

3. Cut fabric or felt into a rectangle the same size as the front of the box.

4. Attach the fabric at the top of the box with hot glue.

5. Cut a slit up the front of the fabric so that the curtains will part.

6. Tie the curtains to each side with yarn.

7. Decorate the stage as desired.

"Who wants to see the puppet show?" asks Noah. Several children nearby call out that they do. Noah moves some chairs over so that they face the stage. When everyone is in place, he says, "Quiet! The show is about to begin!" The children in the audience stop talking and watch as he begins his show using the animal puppets. It is hard to hear what he is making the puppets say, and several children call out that they cannot hear. Two children move on to something else, but two remain. Noah fumbles and mumbles with the puppets for a few moments before declaring, "The end!" The audience claps, and Noah comes out to give a bow.

Wearable Stage

Materials

Recycled tissue box
Cardboard scrap
Yarn
Decorative paper
Scissors
Hot-glue gun (adult use only)

1. In both ends of the tissue box, cut a hole large enough to fit your hand in.

2. Cut the hole in the top of the box (where the tissue comes out) a little larger.

3. Cut a cardboard piece so that its width is the same as the length of the tissue box and the height is 8 inches plus the height of your box.

4. Attach the cardboard piece to the back of the tissue box using hot glue.

5. Decorate as desired.

6. Punch a small hole in each top corner of the cardboard, and tie yarn so that the stage can be worn like a necklace.

7. Finger puppets or small stick puppets work well with this stage.

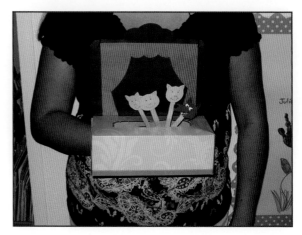

Pillowcase Stage

Materials

Tension rod wide enough to fit across a doorway

Pillowcase or window valance

Scissors

1. Cut the pillow case down each side and across the bottom so that you have two identical pieces. Slide the tension rod through the hem of each piece to create curtains.

2. Hang the curtains in a doorway at the height of the children in your class.

13 Musical Instruments

Isaac and Ben love drums and drumming on objects in their environment. Their teacher wanted to encourage their musical expression, so he created several different drums for the boys to try. Their favorite so far was the 5-gallon-bucket drum. They played and sang familiar songs and then made up their own songs. Ben frequently announced that he was a rock star and was going to play drums to make money when he was a grown-up. After making music during the morning free-choice time, Isaac suggested they take the drums outside to the playground. Another child in the class, Sam, replied, "That is the best idea I've ever heard!"

When somebody turns on the music, it's time to clear some space and spread out—children just cannot help moving and grooving to the beat.

From playing musical instruments to using their whole body to dance to a favorite song, musical experiences are creative outlets for children. Music is a joyful way for children to emotionally express themselves, and it provides many developmental benefits. In addition to the more obvious opportunities for physical development, musical experiences are emotional, cognitive, and mathematical! Playing instruments and dancing are often social collaborations as well. One child beating on a drum can lead to a performance by an entire orchestra. Whether the concert is impromptu or a preplanned activity, musical experiences are a favorite of young children.

INVITING CHILDREN TO EXPLORE MUSICAL INSTRUMENTS

Having a multitude of different types of musical instruments will provide variety in children's experiences and also ensure that there are enough instruments for everyone if an impromptu musical parade happens. You can coordinate songs and music to connect to children's interests and curriculum themes.

MUSIC AND MOVEMENT ACTIVITIES SUPPORT LEARNING ACROSS THE DOMAINS

Music and movement activities promote children's language and literacy development, physical development, social-emotional development, and cognitive development. They can also enhance children's learning of science and math concepts.

Music activities contribute to children's language and literacy development when they sing favorite songs or make up their own words to music. Music may inspire conversations with other children about songs they like. They can explore the rhythms in language as they sing and play instruments. Playing musical instruments provides children with opportunities to enhance their fine motor skills. Dance and creative movement allow children to develop basic locomotor skills, coordination, and balance. As they dance, they build spatial awareness and knowledge of how to control their bodies.

Engaging and cooperating with others when creating music build children's social-emotional skills. They are able to express their emotions with musical instruments and during creative movement. Playing instruments with other children creates opportunities for sharing and taking turns with favored instruments.

Cognitive development as well as science and math learning are supported during music activities as children have the opportunity to make and explore variations in tone. Musical experiences build on children's understandings of beat, rhythm, pattern, and concepts such as fast, slow, loud, and soft.

Many preschool classrooms have a designated area or center for music and movement. The following lists the materials typically included.

- Variety of instruments to shake, strike, and rattle
- Music players
- Scarves and streamers

Create a simple stage by placing a rubber nonskid rug pad on the floor. Place a piece of plywood on the nonskid surface. Voilà! You have a stage.

CREATE SHAKE AND RATTLE INSTRUMENTS

Simple instruments that children can shake or rattle provide opportunities to develop a sense of rhythm and beat.

Potato Masher Rattle

Materials

Potato masher
4 jingle bells

Thin wire, such as
bread-bag ties

1. Tie a jingle bell to a wire.
2. Tie the other end of the wire to the potato masher.
3. Continue, attaching several bells to the potato masher.
4. Encourage the children to shake the masher to make music.

Fruit Cup Shakers

Materials

Recycled fruit cups
Pony beads
Decorative tape

Hot-glue gun
(adult use only)

1. Place a pony bead in a fruit cup.
2. Run a thin bead of glue around the top edge, and place another fruit cup upside down on top.
3. Add decorative tape to cover the seam.

Thrifty Teacher's Guide to Creative Learning Centers

Plastic Bottle Maraca

Materials

Small recycled plastic bottle

Pony beads

Cardboard tube

Duct tape

Hot-glue gun (adult use only)

1. Place a pony bead in a plastic bottle and screw on the lid.

2. Turn the bottle upside down, and insert the cap end into a cardboard tube.

3. Secure the bottle in the tube with hot glue.

4. Wrap the tube in duct tape to create a handle.

Bottle Cap Shaker

Materials

Recycled metal bottle caps

Y-shaped branch

Thin wire

Nail

Hammer (adult use only)

1. Use a hammer and nail to make a hole in the center of each bottle cap.

2. String the caps onto the thin wire.

3. Tie each end of the wire to a prong of the branch.

Joshua finds the maracas in a basket. He carries them around the room, sometimes shaking them quickly and sometimes shaking them slowly. When he approaches some children in the block area, he shakes them fast right in the middle of the group. He does not get much of a reaction, so he moves on. He stops to look out the window. He continues to shake the maracas, but his attention seems to be focused on the children outside. A few moments later, he turns and walks back across the room shaking the maracas in a rather slow and deliberate manner. When he passes a child at the sink, he again shakes them rapidly in her direction. Eventually, he sets the maracas aside when he decides to do a puzzle.

Plastic Egg Maracas

Materials

Plastic eggs

Pony beads or small pebbles

Plastic spoons

Decorative tape

Hot-glue gun (adult use only)

1. Place the beads or pebbles inside the plastic eggs.

2. Seal each egg with hot glue.

3. Use hot glue to attach two spoons to each side of an egg and to attach the handles of the spoons together.

4. Wrap the maracas with decorative tape.

Beaded Shaker

Materials

Recycled plastic bottle

Natural twine

Decorative tape

Pony bead

Hot-glue gun (adult use only)

1. Peel the label from the bottle, and cover the area with decorative tape.

2. Place some pony beads inside the bottle.

3. Screw on and seal the cap using hot glue.

4. Tie twine around the top of the bottle and secure with hot glue.

5. String pony beads onto a long length of twine. **Tip:** Tie a knot in the end of the twine so the beads do not fall off.

6. Wrap the twine around the bottle, interlacing it to make a loose netting. The netting should be a little loose so that it will make noise as the bottle is shaken.

7. Use hot glue to attach the netting in random places.

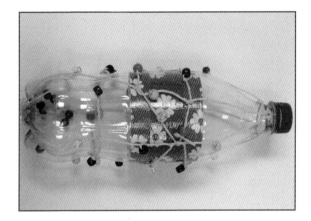

Bell Rattle

Materials

Recycled lint-roller handle

Small bells

Thin wire

1. Thread the wire through the loops at the ends of the bells.

2. Tie the bells to the top of the roller handle using the wire.

Seashell Twirler

Materials

Recycled lint roller

Seashells with small predrilled holes
  (These can be found at craft stores.)

Plastic twine

Duct tape

Scissors

Hot-glue gun (adult use only)

1. Cut four 6-inch pieces of plastic twine.

2. Tie three seashells to each piece of twine.

3. Tie all four pieces together at the top.

4. Drape the seashell strings over the top of the
   lint roller so that the pieces of twine are
   equally spaced.

5. Secure the seashell strings at the top with
   hot glue.

6. Wrap duct tape around the top for added
   durability and to cover the glue.

7. Children can twirl the instrument using
   the handle.

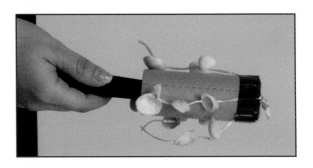

Spoon Rattle Drum

Materials

Plastic or wooden spoon

Drill or hammer and nail (adult use only)

Plastic twine

Pony beads

Scissors

1. Make two holes side by side in the center of
   the spoon using a drill or hammer and nail.

2. Cut two 6-inch pieces of plastic twine.

3. Tie several pony beads onto one end of each
   piece of plastic twine, leaving approximately a
   half inch between each bead.

4. Lace the string through one hole in the spoon.

5. Tie several pony beads onto the twine on the
   opposite side of the spoon.

6. Repeat with the other piece of twine.

7. Children can play this instrument by holding it
   between their hands and rubbing their hands
   back and forth.

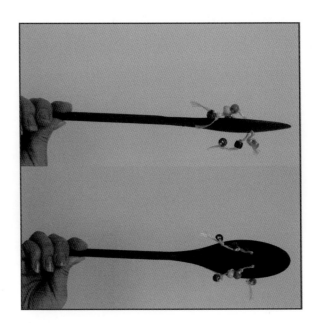

Ribbon Spool Cabasa

Materials

Recycled lint roller

Empty plastic ribbon spool

String of beads

Sandpaper

Hot-glue gun (adult use only)

1. Attach sandpaper around the core of the ribbon spool using hot glue.

2. Attach one end of the bead string to the top inside of the spool using hot glue.

3. Loosely wrap the bead string around the spool.

4. Attach the end of the string at the bottom end of the spool using hot glue.

5. Insert the lint roller into the spool, and secure it with hot glue.

6. Children can play the instrument by rolling it across their palm.

MATERIALS IN ACTION— LEARNING FROM OTHERS

Bobby and Marcus are in the music area of their classroom playing with the instruments. They bang the drums and shake the tambourines. Bobby finds the rattle drum and begins shaking it back and forth. "That's not how you do it!" says Marcus. He yanks it out of Bobby's hand to show him, but Bobby immediately grabs it back. "Hey! I just wanted to show you!" says Marcus. Bobby hands it back. Marcus places the handle of the spoon between his palms and begins rolling it back and forth, which causes the beads to swing. "I want to try! Give it back to me!" says Bobby. He grabs it and gets it positioned between his palms the way Marcus did it. "Now do this!" says Marcus, mimicking the action with his empty hands. Bobby imitates the movement and the beads start swinging.

Chopstick Rattles

Materials

Jingle bells or food-pouch caps

Chopsticks

Plastic twine

Hot-glue gun (adult use only)

Duct tape

1. Cut several short pieces of twine.

2. Tie either a jingle bell or a food-pouch cap to each.

3. Attach the opposite end of each piece of twine to the top of the chopstick using hot glue.

4. Wrap duct tape around the top for added durability and to cover the glue.

Variation: Use recycled bread twist ties or craft wire to attach the jingle bells to the chopstick.

CREATE TAMBOURINES, CYMBALS, AND SLIDERS

Ribbon Spool Tambourine

Materials

Empty cardboard ribbon spool

Chenille stem

Jingle bells

Hot-glue gun (adult use only)

Decorative paper or duct tape

1. Thread and twist the jingle bells onto a chenille stem.

2. Wrap the chenille stem around the spool, and attach it using hot glue.

3. Decorate as desired.

Paper Plate Tambourine

Materials

Heavyweight paper plates	Hot-glue gun (adult use only)
Gravel	Decorative tape
	Markers

1. Place the gravel in one plate.

2. Run a bead of hot glue around the edge of the plate, and attach a second plate facedown.

3. Wrap the edges with decorative tape for added durability.

4. The children can decorate the tambourine with markers.

Strainer Tambourine

Materials

Strainer

Plastic twine

Jingle bells

1. Cut several 4-inch pieces of twine.

2. Tie a jingle bell to one end of each piece.

3. Tie the other end of each piece to the strainer.

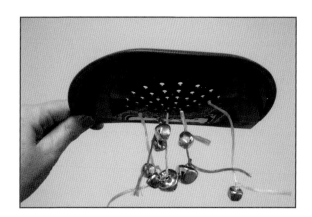

Plastic Lid Castanets

Materials

2 identical recycled plastic lids

Duct tape

Card-stock scraps

Scissors

1. Cut the card stock into a rectangular strip that will fit across your finger.

2. Cut a strip of duct tape that will cover the card-stock strip and leave a half inch on either side.

3. Attach the strip to the lid.

4. Repeat to make a holder for the other lid.

Paint-Edger-Tool Sand Block

Materials

2 paint edger tools

Sandpaper

Scissors

Hot-glue gun (adult use only)

1. Peel the spongy top off of the paint edger tools.

2. Cut sandpaper to fit on the edger tools.

3. Attach the sandpaper using hot glue.

4. Children can play the instrument by rubbing the two pieces together.

Pie-Tin Cymbals

Materials

Aluminum pie tins

Duct tape

1. Cover the edge of the pie tin with duct tape.

2. These instruments can be played with or without drumsticks.

CREATE DRUMS AND SOUND TUBES

Collect a variety of items to use as drumsticks: wooden spoons, unsharpened pencils, sticks, chopsticks, cardboard tubes, and wooden dowels.

Cardboard Can Drum

Materials

Recycled oatmeal container or other cardboard can

Paper towel

Clear contact paper

Hot-glue gun (adult use only)

Hole punch

Scissors

Thin ribbon

Duct tape

1. Cut the paper towel into a circle that will cover the open top of the cardboard can and hang approximately 2 inches down the sides.
2. Cover the paper towel with clear contact paper.
3. Punch holes around the edges that are hanging down the sides.
4. Lace ribbon through the holes.
5. Attach the ribbon on the bottom with hot glue.
6. Cover the bottom and bottom edge of the can with duct tape.

Tin Can Drum Set

Materials

Recycled #10 tin can

Recycled tin cans of assorted sizes

Sandpaper

Duct tape

Hot-glue gun (adult use only)

1. Sand any rough edges on the can openings with sandpaper, or cover the edges with duct tape.
2. Place the #10 can on a flat surface open-end up.
3. Place the other cans around the #10 can until they are configured as desired.
4. Attach cans together using hot glue.
5. Wrap the outer edges using duct tape.
6. Turn the instrument over.

Thunder Tubes

Materials

Paper-towel tube   Balloon

Metal spring   Duct tape

Hole punch   Decorative paper

Scissors   Hot-glue gun

Pencil   (adult use only)

Cardboard scrap

1. Trace around one end of the tube onto the cardboard.

2. Cut out the circle.

3. Attach the spring to the center of the circle using hot glue.

4. Use a hole punch to make five holes around the bottom of the tube.

5. Slide the spring into the end of the tube until the cardboard meets the tube.

6. Use hot glue to attach the cardboard circle to the tube.

7. Cut the opening end off the balloon and discard.

8. Tightly wrap the balloon over the other end of the tube on the end opposite the punched holes.

9. Secure with duct tape.

10. Decorate as desired.

11. Children can play the instrument by shaking the tube.

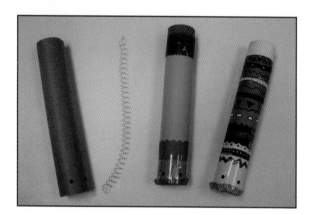

MATERIALS IN ACTION—RHYTHMIC PATTERNS

Maya frequently enjoys the various types of drums that she finds in her classroom. This week, the teacher has added two upside-down, 5-gallon buckets and wooden spoons to the music center. As soon as Maya discovers them, she begins playing the drums by banging the spoons to her own rhythm. For a while, she bangs both spoons down at the same time in a consistently timed manner. Then she begins alternating the bangs—right, left, right, left. She then goes back to joint bangs. This pattern of going back and forth continues for a while. She moves the spoons to the table to continue the beat, but other children protest so she moves back to the buckets.

Rain Stick

Materials

Wrapping-paper tube   Decorative contact
Aluminum foil   paper
Pebbles   Scissors

1. Cut two circles from the contact paper with a diameter that will cover the end of the tube plus 2 inches.

2. Cover one end of the tube with one of the circles.

3. Cut a piece of aluminum foil the length of your tube.

4. Scrunch the aluminum foil so that you can slide it into the tube.

5. Pour approximately one cup of pebbles into the tube.

6. Cover the other end of the tube with the remaining circle of contact paper.

7. Wrap the entire tube with contact paper.

8. The instrument will mimic the sound of rain when the children turn the stick over slowly.

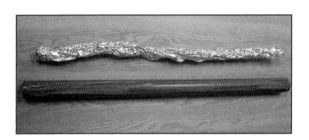

COLLECT AND CREATE MOVEMENT AND DANCE PROPS

Provide a variety of bandanas and scarves for the children to use as they move.

Curtain Ring Pompoms

Materials

Plastic shower-curtain rings
Ribbon
Scissors

1. Cut the ribbon into desired lengths.

2. Tie the ribbons to a curtain ring.

3. Repeat with the other rings and ribbon.

Cardboard Tube Microphone

Materials

Cardboard tube

Recycled paper

Aluminum foil

Duct tape

Hot-glue gun (adult use only)

1. Wad the paper into a ball that will fit on top of the tube without sliding in.

2. Attach the paper ball to the top of the tube with hot glue.

3. Wrap aluminum foil over the ball, and attach the foil to the tube with duct tape.

Washer Tap Dancing

Materials

Large metal washers

Thin elastic

Scissors

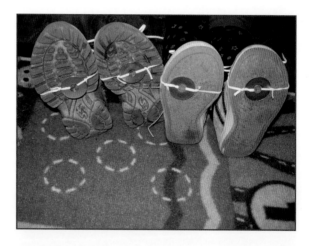

1. Cut two lengths of elastic.

2. Tie one end of each of the elastic bands onto a washer.

3. Wrap the elastic bands around a child's shoe, placing the washer at the bottom of the shoe.

4. Tie the elastic bands at the top of the shoe.

Nina and Daniel are dancing around with scarves to the upbeat music playing on the CD player. Nina appears to be the leader as she is giving directions that Daniel seems to follow. She encourages him to wave the scarf high, then low, then to twirl around. Nina acts dizzy and falls down laughing. When she gets up, she tells Daniel to let the scarf blow in the wind and says that it is really windy because a storm is coming. She makes swishing sounds as she twirls around in the "wind." Daniel follows along as the wind turns into a whirling tornado.

Ponytail-Holder Jingle Bracelets and Anklets

Materials

Ponytail holders

Jingle bells

Fishing line

1. Tie jingle bells to ponytail holders using fishing line.

2. Encourage the children to wear the bracelets and anklets as they move.

References

Copple, Carol, and Sue Bredekamp, eds. 2009. *Developmentally Appropriate Practice in Early Childhood Programs Serving Children from Birth through Age 8.* 3rd ed. Washington, DC: NAEYC.

Cuffaro, Harriett. 1995. "Block Building: Opportunities for Learning." *Exchange* (103): 36–38.

Derman-Sparks, Louise, and Julie Edwards. 2010. *Anti-Bias Education for Young Children and Ourselves.* Washington, DC: NAEYC.

Doctoroff, Sandra. 2001. "Adapting the Physical Environment to Meet the Needs of All Young Children for Play." *Journal of Early Childhood Eduction* 29(2): 105–109.

Erikson, Erik. 1963. *Childhood and Society.* Rev. ed. New York: Norton.

Frost, Joe, Sue Wortham, and Stuart Reifel. 2012. *Play and Child Development.* 4th ed. Boston, MA: Pearson.

Giles, Rebecca, and Karyn Tunks. 2010. "Children Write Their World: Environmental Print as a Teaching Tool." *Dimensions of Early Childhood* 38(3): 23–30.

Guilford, Joy. 1957. "Creative Abilities in the Arts." *Psychological Review* 64(2): 110–118.

Hirsh-Pasek, Kathy, Roberta Golinkoff, and Diane Eyer. 2003. *Einstein Never Used Flashcards: How Our Children Really Learn—and Why They Need to Play More and Memorize Less*. Emmaus, PA: Rodale.

McLoyd, Vonnie. 1983. "Class, Culture, and Pretend Play: A Reply to Sutton-Smith and Smith." *Developmental Review* 3(1): 11–17.

McLoyd, Vonnie. 1986. "Scaffolds or Shackles? The Role of Toys in Preschool Children's Pretend Play." In *The Young Child at Play: Review of Research,* Vol. 4. Washington, DC: NAEYC.

Moore, Gary. 2002. "Designed Environments for Young Children: Empirical Findings and Implications for Planning and Design." In *Children and Young People's Environments*. Dunedin, NZ: University of Otago.

Neuman, Susan, and Kathleen Roskos. 1997. "Literacy Knowledge in Practice: Contexts of Participation for Young Writers and Readers." *Reading Research Quarterly* 32(1): 10–32.

Nicholson, Simon. 1971. "How Not to Cheat Children: The Theory of Loose Parts." *Landscape Architecture* 62(10): 30–34.

Prescott, Elizabeth. 1987. "The Environment as Organizer of Intent in Child-Care Settings." In *Spaces for Children: The Built Environment and Child Development*. New York: Plenum.

Prescott, Elizabeth. 1994. "The Physical Environment: A Powerful Regulator of Experience." *Exchange* (100): 9–15.

Sutton-Smith, Brian. 1995. *The Ambiguity of Play*. Cambridge, MA: Harvard University Press.

Trawick-Smith, Jeffrey. 1993. *Effects of Realistic, Non-Realistic, and Mixed-Realism Play Environments on Young Children's Symbolization, Social Interaction, and Language*. Paper presented at the annual meeting of the American Educational Research Association, Atlanta.

Trawick-Smith, Jeffrey. 2009. *Science in Support of Play: The Case for Play-Based Preschool Programs*. White paper. Willimantic, CT: The Center for Early Childhood Education, Eastern Connecticut State University. http://www.easternct.edu/cece/files/2013/06/TheCaseforPlayinPreschool.pdf

Trawick-Smith, Jeffrey, Heather Russell, and Sudha Swaminathan. 2011. "Measuring the Effects of Toys on the Cognitive, Creative, and Social-Play Behaviors of Preschool Children." *Early Child Development and Care* 181(7): 909–927.

Van Hoorn, Judith, et al. 2002. *Play at the Center of the Curriculum*. 3rd ed. Upper Saddle River, NJ: Merrill Prentice Hall.

Index

Thrifty Teacher's Guide to Creative Learning Centers